Every

Worship

Susan H. Jones

scm press

Published in 2019 by SCM Press
Editorial office
3rd Floor, Invicta House,
108–114 Golden Lane,
London EC1Y 0TG, UK
www.scmpress.co.uk

SCM Press is an imprint of Hymns Ancient & Modern Ltd
(a registered charity)

Hymns Ancient & Modern® is a registered trademark of Hymns
Ancient & Modern Ltd
13A Hellesdon Park Road, Norwich,
Norfolk NR6 5DR, UK

Prayers from *Common Worship: Services and Prayers for the Church
of England* (2000), *Common Worship Daily Prayer* (2005) and *Common
Worship: Times and Seasons* (2006) are copyright © The Archbishops'
Council and are reproduced by permission.

British Library Cataloguing in Publication data
A catalogue record for this book is available
from the British Library

978 0 334 05755 0

Printed by CPI Group (UK) Ltd

Contents

Preface

I have written this book as an introduction to worship and liturgy in the Church. I have written as someone who has for many years been fed and nourished by the worship of the Anglican Church, first in Wales and now in England.

As Dean of Liverpool Cathedral, I have just journeyed through my first Advent and Christmas experienced in this very special place. Once again I have been reminded of how good liturgy, expressed in word, in music, and in movement helps people to engage with the bigger questions in life, and how it gives a structure to the message of the coming of God's Kingdom.

I have spent most of my ministry encouraging people to reflect and to think about their faith in the context of a learning Church, and in response to their call to discipleship. I hope that this book will enable people to reflect on the history and on the tradition of worship in the Church, so helping them continue to explore who God is for them.

I am grateful to many people who helped shape the experiences and ideas underpinning the book. I am grateful to the Revd Canon Professor Leslie J. Francis who has been my guide and inspiration over many years of friendship. I am also grateful to the many people who, responding to God's call to be disciples of Christ, have challenged me in my own discipleship. I am particularly grateful also to the churches and cathedrals where I have served and where I have been encouraged to think about liturgy and worship, and to explore how liturgy and worship can help inform and underpin our Christian discipleship.

Susan H. Jones

1

What is Public Worship?

Worship and liturgy are at the heart of the Christian community. Christian men, women and children have come together over the centuries to worship God. The aim of this book is to help the disciples of today discern and reflect upon their own call to follow Christ and to worship God. The book draws on the experience of three people, but worship of God is more complex than the interpretation given by three people. So readers are encouraged to bring to the text their own experience and to reflect on their understanding of what it means to worship God.

The book listens to the voices of Paul, a member of a Methodist church, Beth, a cradle Anglican, and Maggie, a member of an evangelical Anglican church who began her Christian journey in a Baptist church. The book reflects on their experience of worshipping in different contexts and through different liturgies and services. It explores why worship is led in a particular way and where different forms of liturgy come from.

Paul worships in a Methodist chapel built at the end of the nineteenth century. Paul is used to the Methodist liturgy. Beth worships in a medieval building that has been altered and added to over the centuries. Beth has been brought up in the Anglo-Catholic tradition. Maggie worships in a multi-purpose Anglican evangelical church built on a housing estate in the sixties. Maggie is used to 'free-worship' of a charismatic nature.

As Paul, Beth and Maggie talk, they begin to recognize that each of them has different ways of worshipping, and use different forms of liturgy. They reflect on these differences and begin to realize that there are many different ways of worshipping God and that the whole idea of worship is complex.

Paul, Beth and Maggie begin their reflections by asking what is meant by Christian worship. White (2000) suggests that Christian worship is not an easy expression to define. Richardson (1993) in *A New Dictionary of Christian Theology* defines worship as:

Worship is thus essentially thanksgiving and praise. It may be offered formally according to fixed rites: ritual is the fixed form of words ordered by authority for specified days or times. Or it may be offered in 'free' worship, i.e. without fixed forms, and perhaps with extempore prayer, in which individuals in the congregation may participate. It may be offered with full ceremonial, i.e. accompanying actions, processions, vestments, genuflection and with choirs and music, as a High

Mass or Sung Eucharist. Or it may be offered with a minimum of ceremonial, or in corporate silence as in a Quaker meeting. But the purpose of all worship is the same: to offer praise to God for his grace and glory. (pp. 605-6)

White (1997, pp. 2–16) defines worship as service to God, mirror to heaven, affirmation, communion, proclamation, the arena of transcendence. White (2000) suggests that 'the best way to determine what we mean by Christian worship is to describe the outward and visible forms of worship by Christians' (pp. 18–19). Burns (2006) suggests that worship is much more than words. It is more than the text on the page of a service book. Worship is about a gathering of people.

The preface to *The Methodist Worship Book* (Methodist Church, 1999) sees worship as 'a gracious encounter between God and the Church … Worship is the work of the whole people of God' (p. vii). It states: 'The Church is called to offer worship to the glory and praise of God. From the earliest days of the Church Christian people have gathered together for this purpose' (p. vii).

The Church of England's *Common Worship* (Church of England, 2000) also talks of the 'challenge to draw the whole community of the people we serve into the worship of God' (p. ix).

Perham (2000), in his *New Handbook of Pastoral Liturgy*, suggests that it is the whole congregation, people and ministers, who come together to worship God.

> The worshippers come, in all their variety, individual people with their own needs and expectations, but as the liturgy begins they become a congregation. They discover their corporate identity as they give glory to God who is the Father of them all. The key to true worship is the participation of the whole congregation. (p. 19)

All three begin to realize that defining worship is not always easy. However, Paul, Beth and Maggie recognize that there are a number of components to worship and various different ways to worship. When looking at the liturgies of the Church they see a structure and that structure suggests that worship includes prayer, praise and adoration, thanksgiving, petition, confession, intercession and exhortations. There is the affirmation of faith spoken through the creeds. There is music expressed in hymns, songs, instrumental music, canticles and psalms. There is the notion of time as developed through the Christian year, the Christian week, the lectionary and the rituals of birth, marriage and death. There is art and architecture.

Burns (2006), in his book *Liturgy*, suggests that 'Scripture and sacrament provide the essential framework of Christian liturgy, the skeleton, which other aspects of liturgy then enflesh, wrap around and form the shape of Christian worship' (p. 13). Paul begins to talk about worship and liturgy being about more than words and he quotes from the preface of *The Methodist Worship Book* (Methodist Church, 1999): 'Worship is not a matter of words alone. It involves not only what we say but also what we do' (p. viii). Beth, on the other hand, quotes from the Church of England's (2002) *New Patterns for Worship* which has these opening words: 'Worship is not worship till you do it' (p. x).

As they continue to explore the idea of worship, they look at where different forms of service come from and what role the churches played throughout the centuries in the development of worship and liturgy (Chapters 2 and 3). They reflect on the role of the Church in the life cycle and how the Church developed liturgies to celebrate the important stages in life, like birth, marriage and death (Chapters 4, 5 and 6). They explore the cycle of the Christian year and the important festivals of Advent, Holy Week, Easter, Ascension and Pentecost (Chapter 8). They reflect on the development of the worship space, its layout and furniture, and what it says about God and about the worshippers. They reflect on the architecture of buildings (Chapter 8). For all three of them worship and liturgy is about more than service books and words. It is about the environment, and about the senses: hearing, sight, smell, taste and touch (Chapters 7 and 9).

2

Exploring the Eucharist

Paul, Beth and Maggie are having a conversation about worship. For Paul worship is about the offering to God of praise, glory and honour in reverence and in love. For Beth worship is the subtle blend of word, song, movement, gesture and silence offered through the Church's liturgies. For Maggie worship is shared with others and is a corporate act of praising God. Paul's understanding of worship has been influenced by his journey in the Methodist Church; Beth's has come through her experience of being in the Anglo-Catholic tradition; and Maggie has been influenced in worship by her conversion to faith in the Baptist Church and now lived out in the local Anglican church.

Paul, Beth and Maggie attend churches where the Eucharist (known by different traditions as the Lord's Supper, the Holy Eucharist, the Divine Liturgy, the Holy Mysteries, and the Mass) is celebrated regularly. White (2000) in his chapter on the Eucharist suggests that:

The Eucharist is the most distinctive structure

of Christian worship. It is also the most widely used form of worship among Christians, being celebrated daily and weekly in thousands of congregations and communities all over the world. (p. 229)

TO DO

Draw a map or note down:

What is your experience of worship in church?

What is important to you in worship?

How have you come to worship in the way you do?

In Beth's church they have a daily communion and she tries to make it her discipline to attend as often as she is able to. Paul, on the other hand, receives communion less frequently in his Methodist chapel and only when the minister of word and sacrament is present, which is usually twice a month. Maggie receives communion once a month when the local priest attends the multi-purpose church on the housing estate where she worships.

Paul, Beth and Maggie are exploring together their understanding of the Eucharist. They have looked at the various liturgies of the churches and recognize that there are many similarities in the Eucharist liturgies. To start at the beginning, they have decided to look at the biblical roots of the Eucharist.

The Bible and the Eucharist

Paul, Beth and Maggie discuss the biblical roots of the Eucharist and are aware that while the Eucharist is celebrated because Jesus shared the last supper with his disciples, the background to the Eucharist is set in a Jewish context. They reflect on the fact that in the Synoptic Gospels the last supper was a Passover meal. John's Gospel, however, does not follow this understanding. In John's Gospel Jesus died as the Passover lamb was being sacrificed, which would suggest the previous day for the meal (Bradshaw, Giles, and Kershaw, 2002, p. 99).

Paul, Beth and Maggie reflect that it was during the time of the Passover festival that Jesus inaugurated the last supper: 'He said to them, "I have eagerly desired to eat this Passover with you before I suffer"' (Luke 22.15). White (2000) suggests that Jesus deliberately used 'the climactic occasion of the Jewish year to establish the new covenant' (p. 232) and that Jesus followed the conventional re-enactment of the original Passover meal as commemoration of deliverance from captivity in Egypt.

Paul thinks of the occasions when he has attended the Seder meal in his local Methodist church on Maundy Thursday and he sees the parallels. He remembers the special food, the roast lamb, the green herbs, the bitter herbs, the salt water, the matzos and the red wine. Paul then talks about the actions during which special food is eaten, bread is broken and cups of wine are shared, and he begins to compare them with the institution narratives from the Eucharist in the Bible.

TO DO

Look up Mark 14.22–25 and Matthew 26.26–29. Note down the similarities and differences in the two institution narratives.

Look up 1 Corinthians 11.23–26 and Luke 22.15–20. What are the similarities between these two passages?

Maggie, with her Baptist roots, recognizes that there are two parallel sets of institution narratives in the New Testament, working with the idea that the Last Supper was at the time of the Passover meal. Mark 14.22–25 and Matthew 26.26–29 are quite similar, while 1 Corinthians 11.23–26 and Luke 22.15–20 have strong similarities. White (2000) argues that all accounts, especially the Lucan narrative, are oriented towards the end time, in looking forward to the coming Kingdom of God (p. 233).

The apostle Paul in 1 Corinthians 11 talks of the tradition as something he has received from the Lord and which he is to pass on to future disciples. This tradition, as given by Paul, contains the command to 'Do this in memory of me.' The Eucharist is the memorial of Christ's Passover (Kelly, 1999).

Maggie and Paul reflect on what Beth has said and think about the night on which Jesus was betrayed –Maundy Thursday, the night of the Passover meal. They recognise from their churches' liturgies that Jesus gave thanks over the bread and wine and identified himself with the food that would be shared by his followers: 'This is my body'; 'This is my blood'. They also hear again the command of Jesus to his followers to do this in memory of him.

The New Testament gives brief insight into the first-century celebration of the Eucharist and it is the apostle Paul who raises concerns about 'unworthy partaking of the Lord's supper' (White, 2000). Up until around the year 135 Christians were gathering to take part in a full meal with a separate bread and cup ritual. The meal itself was generally called the 'Lord's supper' (*kyriakon deipnon*) or the 'love feast' (*agapé*), and the bread and cup ritual was called either by the Jewish term 'the breaking of the bread' or by the Greek term 'eucharist' (*eucharistia*), meaning 'thanksgiving' (White, 1997, p. 109).

Paul remembers participating in an *agapé* meal at university with his Catholic friends. He reflects on the sharing of a meal together before receiving bread and wine as symbols of Christ's Last Supper meal with his disciples. He could not participate in the

Catholic Mass because he was not Catholic, but he remembers feeling so much a part of the community when they shared the meal together.

TO DO

Read the following passages from Luke's Gospel: 9.10–17; 21.14–19; 24.13–35.

What, if any, are the common features in the texts that help us understand the Holy Communion service?

Have you ever experienced Holy Communion in the context of a meal, sometimes called an *agapé*? What were the advantages and disadvantages of worshipping in this way?

Having thought about the Bible and the Eucharist, Paul, Beth and Maggie decide to look at how the Eucharist developed in the post-biblical period.

The history of the Eucharist

By the second century the Eucharist had been separated from the complete meal eaten in the evening and was celebrated in the morning. The eucharistic action was preceded by a liturgy of the word with prayers. There would be readings from the Old Testament and from writings that would eventually form the New Testament, and the president would preach. Intercessions followed and the peace was shared before the bread and wine was brought forward. The president would then take the bread and wine, give thanks and break the bread. These were then distributed to the people present or taken to those who could not be present. The *First Apology* of Justin Martyr (AD c 65) gives the first outline of the Eucharist (Bradshaw, Giles and Kershaw, 2002, p. 100; White, 2000, p. 236).

> On the day we call the day of the sun, all who live in the city or the countryside assemble, and the memoirs of the apostles or the writings of the prophets are read for as long as time permits.
>
> When the reader has finished, he who presides over those who have gathered together addresses us, admonishing us to imitate these splendid things.
>
> Then we all stand together and pray and, as we have said earlier, when we have finished praying bread, wine and water are brought up. He who presides offers prayers of thanksgiving (makes Eucharist), according to his ability, and the people give their assent with an 'Amen!' Next the gifts which have been eucharised are distributed, and each one shares in them, and they are also taken, by the deacons to those who are absent. (Justin, *First Apology*, 67, 3–5)

Roughly a century later, in *The Apostolic Tradition* (formerly attributed to Hippolytus), there is an account of the celebration of the Eucharist at Rome. For the first time there is a developed liturgical prayer, which forms the basis of today's eucharistic prayers. After the conversion of Constantine in the fourth century, Christianity became the state religion. The Holy Communion became an elaborate ceremony with processions, vestments and chants. The meaning behind the service developed in the light of the Arian controversy and other heresies of the fourth century, which tended to deny that Christ was fully divine. As a consequence great emphasis was placed on the divinity of Christ. This led to a growing reverence for Holy Communion, which in turn led to people receiving bread and wine less and less frequently until they gave up receiving them altogether.

Beth, whose understanding of the Eucharist is seen from an Anglo-Catholic perspective, talks about her experience of Holy Communion and the way in which there is a reverence in the celebration of communion through wearing vestments, ringing bells, burning incense and venerating the bread and wine. Paul as a Methodist and Maggie as a Baptist, however, talk about their understanding of keeping Holy Communion special by receiving communion less frequently so that it was special when they did receive it.

The Middle Ages saw two main changes in how the Eucharist was celebrated. The first was the growth in private masses and the second was the saying of the Mass in Latin, which was not the language of the people. The celebration of the liturgy then became a religious performance to watch and listen to rather than a liturgy in which to participate (Earey, Gay and Horton, 2001, p. 77). By the end of the Middle Ages most communicants were receiving the sacrament only about twice a year and were passive observers at the Mass for the rest of the time. More and more private masses were being offered, behind screens, inaudibly and secretly.

During the Middle Ages there emerged different understandings of the words of institution (this is my body/blood). In what sense were the bread and wine Jesus' body and blood? Some theologians took the words in a spiritual sense: Christ was spiritually present in the bread and wine, and the sacrament was a sign of the spiritual world, but the bread and wine remained bread and wine. Others believed that after the consecration the real flesh and blood of Christ was physically present on the altar: the same flesh and blood that Jesus had assumed when he became a human being.

The different understandings of the Eucharist and the abuses in the Church came to a head in the Reformation in the sixteenth century. The Eucharist, originally a sacrament of unity, had become a sign of deep divisions, which remain in the Christian Church to this day (Maloney, 1995, p. 151). The Reformation came about in reaction to medieval teaching and practice. The reformers questioned the practice of saying masses for the dead, and advocated using the vernacular and sharing the chalice with the laity. The reformers also opposed the understanding of the sacrifice of the Mass and maintained that 'there was no offering of Christ to the Father in the Eucharist only the sacrifice of oneself, with thanks and praise, through Christ to the Father' (Bradshaw, Giles and Kershaw, 2002, p. 102). In order to suppress the practice of private masses, the reformers insisted that there had to be both a priest and a member of the congregation present to celebrate the Eucharist, and both needed to receive the bread and the wine.

These reformers brought different theological perspectives to the debates surrounding the Eucharist. Like Paul, Beth and Maggie, they had varied understandings of what was happening in the Eucharist. The reformers debated and discussed their understanding of the real presence of Christ in the Eucharist. Luther, for example, did not believe in the traditional doctrine of transubstantiation; he believed in the real, objective presence of Christ in the bread and wine. Luther believed in consubstantiation–that the substance of bread and wine remained alongside the substance of body and blood.

Paul and Maggie find these different terminologies of transubstantiation and consubstantiation difficult to understand. They believe that they have a much simpler understanding of the Eucharist. They find it difficult to comprehend the idea of the sacrifice of the Mass and seem to relate more to the ideas of Ulrich Zwingli, a Swiss leader of the Reformation. Zwingli disagreed with Luther; for him, Christ intended the eucharistic elements 'to signify his body and blood in the midst of an act of memorial' (Bradshaw, Giles and Kershaw, 2002, p. 102). John Calvin also rejected Luther's understanding but he was not as radical as Zwingli. For Calvin, Christ offers himself in communion and is received in faith.

The Reformation in England took these different theological perspectives and through Thomas Cranmer blended them. Cranmer rejected transubstantiation and the sacrificial nature of the Eucharist, maintaining that the bread and wine remained as such, before, during and after consecration. For Cranmer it was the reception that was important. When the bread and wine were received in faith Christ became really present (Bradshaw, Giles, and Kershaw, 2002). His reform began in 1547 with the decision that the readings, creed, Lord's Prayer and commandments were to be read in English. Later in the same year Parliament decided that communion should be received in both languages and eventually the whole service was conducted in English. Cranmer produced prayer books in 1548, 1549, 1552 and 1559. These culminated in *The Book of Common Prayer* of 1662 (Cummings, 2013).

Maggie has seen in the church she attends some old 1662 prayer books and has also come across the 1928 proposed revision of *The Book of Common Prayer* together with a number of service books published between 1966 and 1979: *Alternative Services: Series One*, *Series Two*, and *Series Three*. Beth remembers seeing *The Alternative Service Book 1980*, which was the prayer book that went alongside *The Book of Common Prayer*.

Paul seems to remember his grandfather saying that the early Methodists worshipped in the local parish church according to *The Book of Common Prayer* 1662, especially for the sacrament of Holy Communion, but they also attended their own preaching service. The preaching service gave them the experience of biblical exposition, deep fellowship and vibrant hymn singing.

> **TO DO**
>
> Look at the Eucharist service in *The Book of Common Prayer* 1662 of the Church of England and compare it to the Eucharist service in *Common Worship*.
>
> What differences to you notice in terms of structure, language and eucharistic theology?

The structure of the Eucharist service

As Paul, Beth and Maggie continue to reflect on the Eucharist they start to think of the structure of the service and they recognize a similarity in structure across the denominations. The structure of the Eucharist was the same in many of the mainstream denominations and that structure goes back to the description given by Justin Martyr.

Looking at the whole service, Paul is keen to emphasize that the service of Holy Communion has two main sections: the liturgy of the word and the liturgy of the sacrament. For him the liturgy of the word is centred on the pulpit or the lectern, while the liturgy of the sacrament takes place around the altar or, as Paul calls it, the 'holy table'. These central sections are preceded by the gathering, and then after communion concluded by the dismissal.

Paul, Beth and Maggie discuss the reasons for their

different understanding of whether the ministry of the sacrament takes place on an 'altar' or on a 'holy table'. They reflect on the theological understanding this brings. Beth prefers to call it an altar. Having been brought up in the Anglo-Catholic tradition the word altar is more natural to her; she sees it as the place where the sacrifice of Christ upon the cross is remembered or 'offered'. Maggie prefers holy table because she wants to emphasize the unrepeatable and all-sufficient sacrifice of Christ made 'once for all upon the cross'. For Maggie the use of the word table stresses the notion that Holy Communion is primarily a fellowship meal, the Lord's Supper, at which she recalls a sacrifice, but one that was offered in another place at another time (Earey, Gay and Horton, 2001).

TO DO

Thinking about the language you use to describe the Eucharist, how would you describe the table on which the ministry of the sacrament takes place? Do you prefer holy table or altar?

Why do you prefer to describe it in this way?

Despite their differences in terminology in describing the altar or holy table, Paul, Beth and Maggie come back to the fact that the structure of all the services is similar.

There is a gathering rite, which includes the opening greeting: 'In the name of the Father and of the Son and of the Holy Spirit. Amen.' People are coming together to worship as a Christian community and the worship is offered in the name of God and to God's glory. Following the greeting, 'The Lord be with you,' is the prayer of preparation and penitence. Part of the preparation comes through penitence. In the prayers of penitence people confess that they have sinned against God and neighbour.

> Almighty God, our heavenly Father,
> we have sinned against you
> and against our neighbour
> in thought and word and deed,
> through negligence, through weakness,
> through our own deliberate fault.
> We are truly sorry and repent of all our sins.
> For the sake of your Son Jesus Christ
> who died for us,
> forgive us all that is past
> and grant that we may serve you in newness of life
> to the glory of your name. Amen.
> (*Common Worship*, 2000)

The absolution comes next and reminds the people that God forgives all who repent of their sins.

May almighty God have mercy upon you,
forgive you your sins, and bring you to everlasting
  life
through Jesus Christ our Lord. Amen
(*Common Worship*, 2000)

The *Gloria*, an ancient hymn of praise, is sung. The gathering rite ends with the collect, as all the private prayers of the people are brought together.

The liturgy of the word begins with readings, one from the Old Testament and one from the New Testament, a Psalm and the Gospel. The Gospel, the good news of Jesus, is the culmination of all the readings. Beth reflects with Paul and Maggie on the ceremony that surrounds the Gospel reading in her church. There is a procession where the Gospel is carried to the centre of the church. One person leads with a processional cross, followed by two candle bearers or acolytes, and on special occasions they have incense to cense the Gospel book.

The sermon follows, and Paul reflects that for him this is the most important part of the service as the preacher expounds the readings. His experience is of a sermon that tends to last longer than in the church Beth attends.

After the readings from Scripture and the sermon, the liturgy of the word concludes with the creed and with the prayers of intercession. The creed brings the faith of the people together in a corporate declaration of what they believe. The prayers of intercession are offered by the people. Maggie reflects on her experience of offering the prayers of the people and the opportunity this gives her to bring the concerns of the world, the people and the Church before God.

> The liturgy of the sacrament begins with the peace.
>
> Christ is our peace.
> He has reconciled us to God in one body by the cross.
> We meet in his name and share his peace.
> The peace of the Lord be always with you
> **and also with you**.
> (*Common Worship*, 2000)

The peace acts as a 'hinge' between the liturgy of the word and the liturgy of the sacrament. The peace reminds us that we need to be reconciled before we approach the altar (Earey, Gay and Horton, 2001). For Paul, Beth and Maggie the peace has been contentious in their respective churches as some people have not wanted to participate. The sharing of the peace is, however, a very ancient practice. The apostle Paul talks in his epistles about the kiss of peace, and the peace appears in some of the earliest liturgies of the Church.

After the peace, the table is prepared. Wine, water and bread are brought to the altar along with the monetary offering of the people. Then comes the heart of the service, the prayer of thanksgiving and praise, also known as the eucharistic prayer. This prayer recalls how Jesus himself gave thanks for the bread and wine and the command that this be done by his disciples in remembrance of him.

The eucharistic prayer contains a number of sections, which date back to the earliest centuries of Christian worship. The order of these sections in the Church of England's *Common Worship* varies according to the prayer being used. Eucharistic Prayer B is the one most frequently used in Beth's church, so Paul, Maggie and Beth decide to look closely at its structure. Eucharistic Prayer B begins with three short sentences that demand a response. First there is a mutual greeting, 'The Lord be with you,' followed by an invitation to lift up the heart to God; finally the congregation are asked to 'give thanks to the Lord our God' which is the principal purpose of the eucharistic prayer. The opening sentences are followed with the preface :

Father, we give you thanks and praise
through your beloved Son Jesus Christ, your
   living Word,
through whom you have created all things;

who was sent by you in your great goodness to be
  our Saviour.
By the power of the Holy Spirit he took flesh;
as your Son, born of the blessed Virgin,
he lived on earth and went about among us;
he opened wide his arms for us on the cross;
he put an end to death by dying for us;
and revealed the resurrection by rising to new life;
so he fulfilled your will and won for you a holy
  people.
Short Proper Preface, when appropriate
Therefore with angels and archangels,
and with all the company of heaven,
we proclaim your great and glorious name,
for ever praising you and saying ...
(*Common Worship*, 2000)

The preface is a 'proclamation' of all that God has done,
and why it is that we want to give thanks to God. This
section ends with the *Sanctus* and *Benedictus*. The
Sanctus has been part of the eucharistic prayer since the
fourth century and offers adoration and praise to God.

Holy, holy, holy Lord,
God of power and might,
heaven and earth are full of your glory.
Hosanna in the highest.
(*Common Worship*, 2000)

The *Benedictus* has long been associated with the *Sanctus*, but was removed by Cranmer in 1552 because of its association with the coming of Christ in a physical sense.

> Blessed is he who comes in the name of the Lord.
> Hosanna in the highest.
> (*Common Worship*, 2000)

Earey, Gay and Horton (2001) call the words that follow the *Sanctus* 'the post-sanctus "link" including a preliminary epiclesis' (p. 79). The epiclesis is when the president asks for the coming of God's transforming Holy Spirit.

> Lord, you are holy indeed, the source of all holiness;
> grant that by the power of your Holy Spirit,
> and according to your holy will,
> these gifts of bread and wine
> may be to us the body and blood
> of our Lord Jesus Christ.
> (*Common Worship*, 2000)

In the Eastern Orthodox Church the epiclesis comes towards the end of the eucharistic prayer, as it does in some of the other *Common Worship* eucharistic prayers. In the rites of both the Orthodox and the

Roman Catholic Church this is when the bread and wine is changed and becomes the body and blood of Christ – transubstantiation.

The institution narrative comes next.

> Who, in the same night that he was betrayed,
> took bread and gave you thanks;
> he broke it and gave it to his disciples saying:
> Take, eat, this is my body which is given for you;
> do this in remembrance of me.
>
> In the same way after supper,
> he took the cup and gave you thanks;
> he gave it to them, saying:
> Drink this, all of you;
> this is my blood of the new covenant,
> which is shed for you and for many
> for the forgiveness of sins.
> Do this as often as you drink it,
> in remembrance of me.
> (*Common Worship*, 2000)

The institution narrative varies, as Paul, Beth and Maggie were discovering, but they recognize that it is based on the account in 1 Corinthians and that is rooted in the night that Jesus was betrayed.

Beth then talks with Paul and Maggie about

the *anamnesis*. For Beth this is a key word, but no single English word conveys its full meaning: remembrance, recalling, representation go some way towards capturing the meaning of the word. *Anamnesis*, according to White (2000), 'expresses the sense that in repeating these actions one experiences once again the reality of Jesus himself present' (p. 233).

The congregation responds to the institution narrative with one of the acclamations for Christ's person, for his work and for his expected return.

Great is the mystery of faith.
Christ has died:
Christ is risen:
Christ will come again.
(*Common Worship*, 2000)

The eucharistic prayer then celebrates Christ's sacrifice, made once for all upon the cross, and the people make an offering, a sacrifice of thanks and praise (Earey, Gay and Horton, 2001). The eucharistic prayer moves people on towards receiving communion and asks the Holy Spirit to renew them as they share in communion. The final part of the eucharistic prayer, the doxology, comprises the prayer for unity and praise, as the people are directed and caught up in the worship of heaven.

By whom, and with whom, and in whom,
In the unity of the Holy Spirit,
All honour and glory be yours, almighty Father,
For ever and ever.
(*Common Worship*, 2000)

The people join in the Amen, which affirms the words that have been offered by the president on behalf of the people.

After the Amen comes the Lord's Prayer, the breaking of bread, the invitation to communion, the distribution of communion, the post-communion prayer, the blessing and the dismissal.

Paul, Maggie and Beth reflect on the Eucharist services in *Common Worship* and in *The Methodist Worship Book*. They see a similarity in structure, but notice that the Methodist Church places the creed after the peace in 'Ordinary Season'. Paul speaks about his understanding of Holy Communion being a service of both word and sacrament, but recognizes that John and Charles Wesley saw Holy Communion as a 'divinely appointed means of grace' (Methodist Church, 2003). The fact that when Methodism began people were encouraged to attend the parish church for Eucharist before their own service shows the importance placed upon Holy Communion.

TO DO

Using the Church of England's *Common Worship* Eucharist service Order One and Eucharistic Prayer B, and *The Methodist Worship Book*:

Compare the structure.

Reflect on the differences in the eucharistic prayer wordings.

What do the differences in emphasis tell you about the different theological understanding of the Eucharist?

Conclusion

This chapter has explored the Eucharist service from its early days in the context of an *agapé* meal to the present day. It has investigated the theological changes that have taken place, especially during the Reformation, and reflected on these changes in the light of more modern services of communion. It has also explored the structure of the service in its modern version.

Further reading

Bradshaw, P., Giles, G. and Kershaw, S., 2002, 'Holy Communion', in P. Bradshaw (ed.), *Companion to Common Worship*, pp. 98-147, London: SPCK.

Earey,M.,Gay,P.,and Horton,A.,2001, *Understanding Worship: A Praxis Study Guide,* London:Mowbray.

Kelly, R. B., 1999, *Exploring the Sacraments*, Stowmarket: Kevin Mayhew

Maloney, R., 1995, *The Eucharist*, London: Geoffrey Chapman.

White, J. F., 2000, *Introducing Christian Worship*, Nashville, TN: Abingdon Press.

White, S. J., 1997, *Groundwork of Christian Worship*, Peterborough: Epworth Press.

www.churchofengland.org/prayer-and-worship/ worship-texts-and-resources/common-worship/ holy-communion-0

3

Exploring the Offices

Paul, Beth and Maggie are having a conversation about their commitment to daily prayer and how this reflects patterns of prayer in their different churches. Paul draws on his experience attending a Methodist church, Beth on her experience in an Anglo-Catholic church, and Maggie in an evangelical Anglican church. Together they recognize that Christian communities through the centuries have prayed what have been called variously the Daily (or Divine) Office, the Horarium, the Canonical Hours, and the Liturgy of the Hours (White, 1997). What they are less sure about is the history and development of these offices and in their desire to know more about them they begin by looking at the Bible and daily prayer.

The Bible and daily public prayer

The first Christians seem to have had two main focuses for their worship: the fellowship meal and word-based worship involving Scripture and prayer. This word-based worship would have been taken from the worship patterns of the synagogue and daily prayer that every Jewish family would follow. In the time of Jesus, the core of Jewish daily prayer was the recitation of the confession of faith known as the *Shema Yisrael* (White, 1997). All Jewish males over 12 years of age recited the words 'Hear, O Yisrael: the Lord is our God, the Lord alone...' from Deuteronomy 6.4–5 when getting up from bed and when going to bed. At the beginning and end of the *Shema Yisrael* was a set of benedictions and prayers for the morning and evening. In addition to these private prayers, public worship was held in the synagogue three times a day, in the morning, afternoon and evening. These services included prayers, recitation of psalms and readings from the Torah.

The early Christians would have continued to worship in the synagogue and understood that daily prayer enabled people to reflect on the fact that the day ahead gave potential to reveal God and to make known God's action in the world. While Sunday worship concentrated on God's acts of redemption, daily worship emphasized God's acts of creation (White, 1997). The New Testament contains a number of references to Christians assembling for daily prayer, including the following:

- 'All these were constantly devoting themselves

to prayer'. (Acts 1.14)

- 'Pray without ceasing'. (1 Thessalonians 5.17)
- 'Devote yourselves to prayer, keeping alert in it with thanksgiving'. (Colossians 4.2)

For the first Christians it seems to be implied in the New Testament that every action and every deed could and should become a prayer (Jasper and Bradshaw, 1992). There is, however, very little evidence in the New Testament to suggest a regular gathering for daily prayer.

Beth is used to a daily Eucharist as part of her discipline and has never really thought about the daily offices of the Church. She starts to reflect on the Jewish *Shema Yisrael* and the constant act of praying to God throughout the day. She thinks that it is a good way to begin and end the day, focusing on God and saying the verses from Deuteronomy:

Hear, O Israel: The Lord is our God, the Lord alone. You shall love the Lord your God with all your heart, with all your soul and with all your might. (Deuteronomy 6.4–5)

Having talked about the biblical basis of daily prayer, Paul, Beth and Maggie focus on the historical developments of daily prayer.

> **TO DO**
>
> What is your experience of the daily offices?
>
> Does your church pray daily?
>
> What is the purpose of daily prayer?
>
> What are your reflections on Deuteronomy 6.4–5?

The history of daily public prayer

Dating from late in the first century or early in the second, the Christian treatise the *Didache* advised Christians to pray the Lord's Prayer three times a day. Many early Christians were concerned about the number of times they should pray during the day. One Christian writer, Clement of Alexandria, thought that for true Christians prayer should be prayed constantly throughout their whole lives. He suggested that Christians should gather together for prayers in the morning, at noon, and at the evening meal, and that night prayers should be said in families or in private (White, 1997). Others, including Tertullian and Cyprian, suggested prayer three times a day, which was in line with Daniel's example in the Old Testament (Daniel 6.10).

Maggie tries to pray three times a day, having been taught to do so in the Baptist church she attended.

She tends not to use set formularies. Following Clement of Alexandria, she feels that prayer should be about the whole being and be said throughout the day and throughout life.

The Apostolic Tradition, a treatise written in about AD 217, tells of Christian practice in Rome at the time. It describes seven daily hours of private prayer and a daily gathering for instruction and prayer (White, 2000). Prior to the fourth century, however, no evidence exists for regular daily services (Bradshaw, 1992).

In the late fourth century public worship began to take place on a regular basis. *The Apostolic Constitutions*, written in about AD 375 to 380, instructed Christians to gather together every day in the morning and evening to sing psalms and pray (White, 2000).

Some people, wishing to live the Christian life more intensely, separated themselves from the world and went to live in the desert in imitation of Christ's wilderness experience. Other Christians gathered into smaller groups in order to devote themselves to prayer, communal engagement and acts of charity. Basil the Great gathered such a group around his cathedral and placed them under a Rule of Life, which included instructions for a complex pattern of daily prayer consisting of eight services or hours. These comprised a Vigil at midnight, Matins at cockcrow (2 a.m.), Prime in the early morning, Terce at the third hour (9 a.m.), Sext at the sixth hour (12 noon), Nones at the ninth hour (3 p.m.), Vespers when the day's work was over and Compline at nightfall. Reciting the 150 Psalms was at the centre of this worship (White, 1997).

This practice, known as the people's office, became the ideal for committed men and women. It did not survive long, though, as it required a great deal of time and a high degree of literacy. The saying of the offices came to be left to religious professionals, monks, nuns and ordained ministers.

Beth has little experience of saying the daily office as a community activity because of her work commitments, but she can see how encouraging and enabling it could be to pray with other Christians on a daily basis. She would find it difficult to join with others every day, let alone eight times a day.

The pattern of eight hours of prayer continued through the medieval period. Added to these were special prayers to the Virgin Mary; as people began to believe that she played an essential role in the fate of everyone. There was also a change from the joyful thanksgiving that had infused the people's office to a more penitential service as people began to focus more on death.

It was not until early in the sixth century that a definitive Western pattern of daily prayer emerged. It was Benedict who set the pattern for his monks, and thereafter monasticism and the daily offices evolved together. The daily offices moved away from the life of the ordinary Christian person. Parochial clergy copied the monks by holding eight services daily in the chancels of their churches and the monastic offices became the daily worship.

During the twelfth century a shortened office was developed. The *modernum officium*, used in the papal chapel in Rome, featured an abbreviated lectionary, more hymns and a modified calendar. The birth of the Franciscan order of monks in the following century brought pressure for shorter services and a service that could be used while travelling (White, 2000).

Paul remembers using the Franciscan office while at college. In the college chapel they used *Celebrating Common Prayer* (Society of St Francis, 1992) as part of the daily round of prayers. He favoured the midday prayers as they were short and refocused the day. He was unaware of the history of the Franciscan order and the role they played in influencing the daily offices.During this period the office changed; less Scripture was read and celebrations of the saints increased. The office became more a succession of festival days and less the regular reciting of the Psalter and the reading of Scripture. Practice also changed at this time. The office had developed up to the thirteenth century as a choral office, said and sung together in choir by religious communities and in the churches by priests and minor clergy. With developments in travel and learning, people began to say the office privately. This change allowed a new order of monks, the Jesuits in the sixteenth century, to be free from having to sing the office (White, 2000).

TO DO

Look at one monastic office, for example that of the Franciscans or the Benedictines. How different is their round of services from that proposed in the Early Church?

What types of services do they hold?

How easy or difficult would it be to follow this pattern in daily life?

By the end of the Middle Ages there was widespread dissatisfaction with the divine office. Reform of the liturgy was seen to be needed as it had become too complex. Cardinal Francisco de Quiñones, a Spaniard, produced a breviary reforming the liturgy in 1535, revising this in 1536. Quiñones' breviary retained certain traditional features: for example, it contained all the hours from Vigil to Compline, but they were no longer choral services. It was intended for private use by individual clerics. Quiñones' breviary was later suppressed in 1558, and in 1568 the Roman Breviary began to be used. This remained in use in the Roman Catholic Church until the 1970s.

The reformers brought a renewed understanding of the importance of Scripture and a call for the restoration of a popular form of daily prayer. The first reformed offices to emerge from the Reformation were Lutheran (Cuming, 1992). Martin Luther, however, was conservative in his approach. In 1523 and 1526, he proposed two daily services, Matins and Vespers. These services on weekdays and non-feast days consisted of lessons, psalms, canticles, hymns, the Lord's Prayer, collects, the creed and a sermon. These services were intended for lay people and were used by schools and universities.

John Calvin, Martin Bucer and others produced morning and evening services for public worship. At the centre of these services were the reading and preaching of Scripture; added to these were prayers, vernacular hymns, a canticle and the Lord's Prayer. Martin Bucer, the chief reformer in Strasbourg, in particular developed the daily offices for use in parish churches. He simplified the number of services to two, one in the morning and one in the evening, but kept the structure of the Latin offices and added more Scripture and more exposition (White, 2000).

In Britain the Reformation brought a new prayer book through the work of Archbishop Thomas Cranmer. Cranmer compiled *The Book of Common Prayer* of 1549 and 1552, drawing on the work of the continental reformers and Cardinal Quiñones. Cranmer combined Matins, Lauds and Prime from the medieval English Sarum Breviary into Matins, while Vespers and Compline were condensed into Evensong. In the 1552 edition, the names of these services became Morning Prayer and Evening Prayer.

In the Preface to *The Book of Common Prayer* (1552) Cranmer defined his chief objective: 'the thread and order of Holy Scripture shall be continued entire and unbroken'. Holy Scripture would now be read consecutively in the services. Over the course of a year the Old Testament would be read once and the New Testament three times. Psalms would be repeated on a daily basis and the whole Psalter was covered each month. The services were in English with clear structures and simple rules to follow.

The service now included the Lord's Prayer, versicles (a short sentence sung by a priest or minister and followed by a congregational response), psalms with the *Gloria Patri* ('glory be to the Father', a short hymn of praise to God), two lessons, canticles (a hymn or chant with a biblical text), the *Kyrie* (response to the litany), the creed, the Lord's Prayer (for a second time) and three closing collects (prayers bringing the liturgy to a close). In *The Book of Common Prayer* (1552) a penitential prelude consisting of penitential sentences from Scripture, a call to confession, a general confession and absolution were added. In 1662, additional prayers and provision for an anthem were added at the end of the service (White, 2000). For over 300 years Morning Prayer and Evening Prayer were the normal Anglican services.

Beth remembers her grandmother talking about Sung Matins in her parish church. She thinks about how *The Book of Common Prayer* 1662 has sustained so many people over the centuries and how it still influences the liturgical life of the Anglican Church. She has a brief recollection of attending a Choral Evensong and listening to the versicles and responses written by William Byrd back in the sixteenth century when the liturgies of Morning Prayer and Evening Prayer were being written.

> O Lord, open thou our lips.
> And our mouth shall shew forth thy praise.
> O God, make speed to save us.
> O Lord, make haste to help us.
> Glory be to the Father, and to the Son…
> Praise ye the Lord.
> The Lord's name be praised.
> (*The Book of Common Prayer*, 1662)

She remembers the beauty of this service and the feeling of being transcended to a holy place.

The orders of Morning Prayer and Evening Prayer in *The Book of Common Prayer* had a dual function. They were used both as daily prayer and for the main act of worship on a Sunday. Until the nineteenth century the normal Sunday morning service consisted of Morning Prayer, Litany and Ante-communion.

TO DO

Either:

Listen to a sung service of Evensong and note down the different parts of the service that are sung. How does this compare with *The Book of Common Prayer* (1662)?

Or:

Use Thomas Tallis's or William Byrd's settings of the versicals and responses to reflect on the service of Matins or Evensong.

It was not until the 1928 proposed revision of *The Book of Common Prayer* that a distinction was made between weekday and Sunday services, through a separate provision of psalms and readings. Other changes included the removal of the penitential introduction on weekdays, while a shorter form of it was included as an alternative. The first Lord's Prayer was removed. Invitations for the seasons of the year were included for optional use with the *Venite*. The *Venite* (Psalm 95) is used at the beginning of the day and invites people to worship God and to listen to God's voice.

1   O come, let us sing unto the Lord :

let us heartily rejoice in the strength of our salvation.

2   Let us come before his presence with thanksgiving :

and shew ourselves glad in him with psalms.

3   For the Lord is a great God :

and a great King above all gods.

4   In his hand are all the corners of the earth :

and the strength of the hills is his also.

5   The sea is his, and he made it :

and his hands prepared the dry land.

6   O come, let us worship, and fall down :

and kneel before the Lord our Maker.

7   For he is the Lord our God :

and we are the people of his pasture, and the sheep of his hand.

[8   Today if ye will hear his voice, harden not your hearts :

as in the provocation,

and as in the day of temptation in the wilderness;

9   When your fathers tempted me :

proved me, and saw my works.

10   Forty years long was I grieved with this generation, and said :

It is a people that do err in their hearts,

for they have not known my ways.

11   Unto whom I sware in my wrath :

that they should not enter into my rest.]
Glory be to the Father, and to the Son :
and to the Holy Ghost;
as it was in the beginning, is now, and ever shall
  be :
world without end. Amen.
(*Common Worship: Daily Prayer*, 2005)

In 1927 Psalm 51 was added as an alternative to the
Te Deum. The *Te Deum* was one of a group of early
hymns that praise God the Trinity.

We praise you, O God,
we acclaim you as the Lord;
all creation worships you,
the Father everlasting.
To you all angels, all the powers of heaven,
the cherubim and seraphim, sing in endless
  praise:
Holy, holy, holy Lord, God of power and might,
heaven and earth are full of your glory.
The glorious company of apostles praise you.
The noble fellowship of prophets praise you.
The white-robed army of martyrs praise you.
Throughout the world the holy Church acclaims
  you:
Father, of majesty unbounded,
your true and only Son, worthy of all praise,

the Holy Spirit, advocate and guide.
You, Christ, are the King of glory,
the eternal Son of the Father.
When you took our flesh to set us free
you humbly chose the Virgin's womb.
You overcame the sting of death
and opened the kingdom of heaven to all believers.
You are seated at God's right hand in glory.
We believe that you will come and be our judge.
Come then, Lord, and help your people,
bought with the price of your own blood,
and bring us with your saints
to glory everlasting.
Save your people, Lord, and bless your inheritance.
Govern and uphold them now and always.
Day by day we bless you.
We praise your name for ever.
Keep us today, Lord, from all sin.
Have mercy on us, Lord, have mercy.
Lord, show us your love and mercy,
for we have put our trust in you.
In you, Lord, is our hope:
let us never be put to shame.
(*Common Worship: Daily Prayer,* 2005)

The *Benedicite* was also added, the Song of Creation
that comes from the Prayer of Azariah and the Song
of the Three Holy Children in the Apocrypha.

1   Bless the Lord all you works of the Lord:
sing his praise and exalt him for ever.
2   Bless the Lord you heavens:
sing his praise and exalt him for ever.
3   Bless the Lord you angels of the Lord:
bless the Lord all you his hosts;
bless the Lord you waters above the heavens:
sing his praise and exalt him for ever.
4   Bless the Lord sun and moon:
bless the Lord you stars of heaven;
bless the Lord all rain and dew:
sing his praise and exalt him for ever.
5   Bless the Lord all winds that blow:
bless the Lord you fire and heat;
bless the Lord scorching wind and bitter cold:
sing his praise and exalt him for ever.
6   Bless the Lord dews and falling snows:
bless the Lord you nights and days;
bless the Lord light and darkness:
sing his praise and exalt him for ever.
7   Bless the Lord frost and cold:
bless the Lord you ice and snow;
bless the Lord lightnings and clouds:
sing his praise and exalt him for ever.
8   O let the earth bless the Lord:
bless the Lord you mountains and hills;
bless the Lord all that grows in the ground:
sing his praise and exalt him for ever.

9   Bless the Lord you springs:
bless the Lord you seas and rivers;
bless the Lord you whales and all that swim in the
    waters:
sing his praise and exalt him for ever.
10   Bless the Lord all birds of the air:
bless the Lord you beasts and cattle;
bless the Lord all people on earth:
sing his praise and exalt him for ever.
11   O people of God bless the Lord:
bless the Lord you priests of the Lord;
bless the Lord you servants of the Lord:
sing his praise and exalt him for ever.
12   Bless the Lord all you of upright spirit:
bless the Lord you that are holy and humble in
    heart;
bless the Father, the Son and the Holy Spirit:
sing his praise and exalt him for ever.
(*Common Worship: Daily Prayer*, 2005)

In the Church of England, these alterations were given authority in *Alternative Services: Series One*, Morning and Evening Prayer (1966) for experimental use. *Series Two* followed in 1968 with very little alteration. *Series Three* followed from 1975. These services were substantially the *Series Two* forms in modern language, supplemented by the litany, prayers for various occasions and endings. With some minor changes these forms appeared in *The Alternative Service Book 1980* (Jasper and Bradshaw, 1992). It was another 20 years before the Church of England produced *Common Worship* and its daily prayer.

Of the free churches, Methodism has been closest to the Anglican tradition in respect of the daily offices. As Anglicans, the Wesleys observed the rubrics in *The Book of Common Prayer* of reciting the daily offices, and according to John Wesley Methodist congregations were expected to take part in the worship of their parish churches, their own distinctive service being an addition. After Wesley's death and as Methodists became more independent they were encouraged by Conference to use an abridged form of the Anglican Office.

In *The Sunday Services of the Methodists with other occasional services* (1788), both Morning and Evening Prayer include the Lord's Prayer, said only once, Psalms 100, 98 and 67 replace the canticles, although the *Te Deum* is retained, and the Prayer for All Conditions of Men and the General Thanksgiving are included in the closing prayers. The *Venite* is omitted from Morning Prayer. In 1882 the *Venite* and *Benedictus* were restored, the Prayer of the High Court of Parliament was added to the closing prayers of Morning Prayer, and Evening Prayer was omitted altogether. The Nicene Creed was added as an alternative to the Apostles' Creed, for use when communion was to follow. This version of Morning Prayer was retained in the 1936 *Book of Offices* (Tripp, 1992).

After 1975, Morning Prayer was abandoned by the Methodist Church and in its place the 'Sunday Service' was included in the Methodist Service Book. In *The Methodist Worship Book* (1999) there is provision for daily prayer in the morning and evening, and guidance is given for Morning, Afternoon or Evening Services; with two orders of services provided. These services are seen as the former preaching services.

Paul remembers seeing some of the old prayer books of the Methodist Church in the chapel he attended when he was a boy. His father was a Methodist local preacher; Paul recalls the emphasis in his service plans being on preaching, the rest of the service consisting of hymns, prayers and Scripture readings.

The structure

The modern forms of Morning and Evening Prayer in *Common Worship* follow the structure of a service of the word and allow some flexibility. The services use both *The Alternative Service Book 1980* and the office book of the Society of St Francis, *Daily Office SSF*. The daily office of the Franciscans had a fourfold pattern of prayer – morning, midday, evening and night – and was like the 'cathedral' offices of the Early Church. When it was revised two books were produced, one for SSF use, the other for general use and called *Celebrating Common Prayer* (1992). Some distinctive features of *Celebrating Common Prayer* can be found in the opening prayers, responsories after Scripture readings and the rich variety of canticles in the main volume of *Common Worship* (Dawtry and Headley, 2001).

The orders of Morning and Evening Prayer on a Sunday are a mixture of *The Book of Common Prayer* (1662) services, which were revised in *The Alternative Service Book 1980,* and material from *Celebrating Common Prayer.* The structure of these services consists of the preparation, which includes prayers of penitence, prayer of thanksgiving, opening canticle, opening prayer, the liturgy of the word, including two Bible readings, a psalm and the sermon. Next comes the thanksgiving followed by the conclusion.

In the preparation to the service a greeting is given, the traditional wording being 'O Lord, open our lips'. For Morning Prayer in its modern form the greeting is taken from 1 Timothy 1.2, 'Grace mercy and peace...' and from Psalm 118.24, 'This is the day that the Lord has made... ' At Evening Prayer the greeting, with the words 'The light and peace of Jesus Christ be with you...' and 'the glory of the Lord has risen upon us', comes from *Celebrating Common Prayer.* The greeting may be followed at Morning and Evening Prayer by 'We have come together...'

which is adapted from the opening paragraph in *The Alternative Service Book 1980.*

The prayers of penitence in both Morning and Evening Prayer are introduced with a verse of Scripture, Matthew 4.17. The versicles and responses that conclude these prayers in Morning Prayer come from Psalm 28.7, 9.

The prayer of thanksgiving comes from *Celebrating Common Prayer* and gives thanks for the gift of the light of the day, of lamplight to lighten the darkness and of the light of Christ to illuminate our lives. The 'blessing' form echoes the style of Jewish prayers (Dawtry and Headley, 2001). The opening canticles that round off this first part of the services are optional. In Morning Prayer the *Benedicite* (a song of creation) in its shorter or longer form can be used in Ordinary Time, the *Jubilate* (a song of joy) in festal seasons, the Easter anthems in the Easter season and the *Venite* (a song of triumph) in Advent or Lent. At Evening Prayer the *Phos hilaron* (song of the light) and/or verses from Psalms 141 or 104 can be used. The opening prayer is optional and is based on similar forms from *Celebrating Common Prayer.*

Paul and Maggie recognize the fact that people need to know when a service has started, and the preparation provides space for people to collect their thoughts for the mood and tone of the service. The preparation also helps people to prepare for the liturgy of the word.

In both Morning and Evening Prayer the next part of the service is the Word of God and has two possible shapes. The first option places the psalm and Old Testament canticle at Morning Prayer and the New Testament canticle at Evening Prayer, followed by either one or two readings, an optional responsory, and the Gospel canticle (the *Benedictus* in the morning and the *Magnificat* in the evening). This pattern in its broadest sense is similar to the Benedictine order in the West. The second option is that of *The Book of Common Prayer*, in which the first reading follows the psalm and the second comes before the canticles. The first option emphasizes the office as an act of praise, like the original people's office of the early Christians, and the second makes the readings more prominent (Dawtry and Headley, 2001).

The sermon follows and is mandatory on Sundays, if the service is the principal service of the day, and the Apostles' Creed ends this section of the service on a Sunday. After the sermon one of the four thanksgivings may be used to close the service. These thanksgivings are: thanksgiving for the word, thanksgiving for holy baptism, thanksgiving for the healing ministry of the Church, and thanksgiving for the mission of the Church. Or the service may continue with prayers of intercession, which are broad prayers focusing on the needs of the world. The collect of the day is included at this point, followed by the Lord's Prayer.

The conclusion for both Morning and Evening Prayer ends with a suitable blessing, or with the grace or the peace. The exchange of the peace dates back to the early Christians at the conclusion of common prayer and it formed what they called 'the seal' to their prayers (Dawtry and Headley, 2001).

As they discuss the services of Morning and Evening Prayer, Paul and Maggie reflect that not only does a service require a beginning, it also needs an ending. This may be called the dismissal, as in *The Methodist Worship Book*, or the conclusion as in *Common Worship*, which includes a blessing or the grace or the peace.

Paul also considers the structure of the Morning, Afternoon and Evening Services in *The Methodist Worship Book*. They too have a time of preparation which includes a greeting, a prayer of approach, prayer of adoration, a prayer of confession and declaration of forgiveness. The ministry of the word follows, which includes readings from Scripture and a sermon. This part of the service, like the Anglican service, is rounded off with the creed. Following the creed is what the Methodist Church calls the response and this comprises prayers of thanksgiving and prayers of intercession. The Lord's Prayer ends the prayers. Then comes the dismissal.

Paul is surprised how the two denominations

have very similar services and offer flexibility within the services. Maggie is also surprised that within a set structure there is flexibility, having spent most of her Christian life in churches that don't have set liturgies.

TO DO

Compare the Church of England's *Common Worship* modern form of Morning and Evening Prayer on Sundays with *The Methodist Worship Book* Morning, Afternoon and Evening Services.

Note down the similarities and the differences.

Night Prayer has also been included in *Common Worship* and is taken from Night Prayers on Saturdays in *Celebrating Common Prayer*. The order of Night Prayer originates from the monastic office of Compline. It disappeared as a service in its own right in England at the Reformation, though elements from the service of Compline in the Sarum rite were added into Evening Prayer by Thomas Cranmer. The service reappears in the 1928 proposed prayer book revision and the traditional form of Night Prayer in *Common Worship* is based on this prayer book (Dawtry and Headley, 2001).

Conclusion

This chapter has explored the offices of the Church, both Morning Prayer and Evening Prayer. It has looked at the discipline of the first Christians and their continued association with the Jewish understanding of daily prayer and has explored the subsequent developments of these offices in the Early Church until the present day.

Further reading

Bradshaw, P. (ed.), 2002, *Companion to Common Worship*, Vol. 1, London: SPCK.

Jasper, R. C. D. and Bradshaw, P. F., 1992, *A Companion to the Alternative Service Book 1980*, 4th edn, London: SPCK.

Jones, C., Wainwright, G., Yarnold, E. and Bradshaw P. (eds), 1992, *The Study of Liturgy* London.

White, J., 2000, *Introduction to Christian Worship*, Nashville, TN: Abingdon Press.

White, S. J., 1997, *Groundwork of Common Worship*, Peterborough: Epworth Press.

www.churchofengland.org/prayer-and-worship/

worship-texts-and-resources/common-worship/
daily-prayer

4

Engaging through Baptism

Paul, Beth and Maggie are having a conversation about Christian initiation, commonly called Holy Baptism. Paul was baptized into the Christian Church as a teenager. The service of baptism took place in his local Methodist church, which he had attended since a young child. Beth talks of her baptism as a baby in an Anglo-Catholic church and the influence her grandmother had on her Christian life. Maggie was baptized as an adult and her service was conducted in her local Baptist church with full immersion.

All three of them have attended baptism services over a number of years and have seen a change in people's understanding of what baptism is about. They have observed a movement away from the traditional understanding of baptism as an initiation into the Christian Church, with the implication that baptism is the beginning of a life-long journey in Christ. According to Billings (2004), baptisms, commonly called christenings, are now seen as an epiphany, the 'new wedding' and the cementing of relationships.

As Paul, Beth and Maggie explore the symbolism in the service of baptism, they begin to look back into the history of the Church and the sacrament of baptism. They look first at baptism and the Bible before moving on to the history of baptism in the Early Church.

The Bible and baptism

As Paul, Beth and Maggie begin to talk about the symbolism in the baptism liturgy, they focus on the use of water in the baptism liturgy and they reflect on the fact that water has been a major symbol and ritual for many religions. As Jasper and Bradshaw (1992) comment:

> Water can express cleansing and purification, or refreshment and regeneration. It can be seen as bringing life, since water is necessary for all life; but equally it can be seen as bringing death by drowning, and in some religious myths water symbolizes the chaos before life began, and in others death is a sea from across which no one returns. (p. 323)

As Paul, Beth and Maggie investigate Jewish practice in the Old Testament they see that water was used to cleanse from impurity (Leviticus 12.5–13), while Ezekiel 36.25 talks about God's people being sprinkled with pure water to be made clean in the messianic age (Jasper and Bradshaw, 1992). Pagans who converted to Judaism went through a ritual purification by immersion, in addition to circumcision of the male candidates.

It was against this background that the first Christians adopted baptism as the ritual initiation of new converts into the Christian community. The baptism of repentance for the forgiveness of sins offered by John the Baptist added to the idea of baptism as the first step in becoming a member of the Christian community. The Synoptic Gospels (Matthew 3.13–17; Mark 1.9–11; Luke 3.21–22) all record Jesus' baptism by water and the Spirit and this influenced the theology and ritual of later Christian practice (Jones and Tovey, 2002; Johnson, 2013).

When Paul looks at the Synoptic Gospels he finds there are no accounts of Jesus baptizing, but in John 3.22,26 there is a suggestion that he did. In contradiction of this, John 4.2 seems to state that Jesus, unlike his disciples, did not baptize. Recent New Testament scholars agree that the command in Matthew 28.19 to baptize in the name of the Father, the Son and the Holy Spirit is not an authentic saying of Jesus, but a later post-resurrection addition (Jones and Tovey, 2002).

The act of initiation into the Christian community through a process, that included baptism can be seen in other parts of the New Testament. For example, 1 Peter 3.21 recognizes: 'Baptism … now saves you, not as a removal of dirt from the body, but as an appeal to God for a clear conscience, through the resurrection of Jesus Christ.' Beth discovers that Acts 22.16 reiterates this: 'be baptized, and have your sins washed away, calling on his name'. Beth assumes from this that there was little preparation for those wishing to be baptized and in fact the Acts of the Apostles suggests that there was no delay between an individual's decision to become a Christian and the actual act.

New Testament scholars agree that the act of baptism included a profession of faith, but it is unclear as to whether there was a particular formula, the laying on of hands, or anointing with oil (Johnson, 2013). There is also uncertainty about the baptism of children alongside their parents.

TO DO

Read 1 Peter 3.21 and Acts 22.16.

What does it mean to be saved through baptism?

How in your experience is this notion of being saved part of baptism?

How does the symbolism of water washing away sin help in understanding what baptism is about?

The history of baptism

As Paul, Beth and Maggie continue to investigate baptism, they look at the documentation from the second and third centuries including the writings known as the *Didache* and the work of Justin Martyr. They discover that the *Didache* (also known as *The Teaching of the Twelve Apostles*) forbids those who are unbaptized from participating in the Eucharist. Both the *Didache* and Justin Martyr suggest that those about to be baptized are to fast. Having assented to baptism, they have water poured on them three times with a trinitarian formula, and there is to be a eucharistic celebration.

By the beginning of the third century, Tertullian (an early Christian writer from Carthage in Africa) describes his North African community baptizing children and adults between Easter and Pentecost, although he qualifies this by saying that baptism can take place at any time. For Tertullian the most solemn occasion for baptism is Easter. He speaks of a rigorous preparation including prayers, fasting and all-night vigils (White, 2000). The person who baptizes is normally the bishop, although this can be delegated to a presbyter or deacon. A prayer over the water is followed by a renunciation of the devil and the laying on of the bishop's hands. The person is immersed in water three times, alongside the trinitarian profession of faith, then the candidate is anointed and signed with the cross. The bishop then lays hands on the head of the candidate in blessing, inviting and welcoming the Holy Spirit. The Eucharist follows and the newly baptized receives first communion (Jasper and Bradshaw, 1986).

Paul recognizes the Early Church's form of baptism. His experience in the Methodist Church is that Christian baptism is always administered with water and always 'in the name of the Father, and of the Son and of the Holy Spirit'.

Paul looks to *The Apostolic Tradition* and sees a similar process described. A description is offered of one single celebration of initiation, which encompassed baptism, confirmation and first communion. Jones and Tovey (2002), however, suggest that because of the uncertainty of the real origin of the text it is 'difficult to use it as independent evidence for third-century Roman practice'.

In the fourth century, Christian initiation developed significantly after the conversion of the Emperor Constantine. The large numbers of people coming forward for baptism meant that the preparation and scrutiny of the candidates reduced. Theologically, it was believed that the remission of sins conferred in baptism could only be conveyed once, and so people began to delay baptism for as long as possible in order to be certain of salvation. Consequently many remained as *catechumens*–unbaptized but receiving Christian instruction–for many years.

Later came the move from mainly adult baptism to infant baptism. Waiting for baptism until later in life in order to gain salvation changed to baptizing very soon after birth, to stop babies dying unbaptised. Beth believes in infant baptism and most people she knows were baptized as babies. She has heard people say that once babies are baptized they develop quicker. Maggie, on the other hand, has experience of adult baptism and full immersion. She sees baptism as a commitment to follow Christ and therefore the person has to be able to make the promises. Both, however, agree on recognizing baptism with water and through a trinitarian formula.

The basic pattern of initiation in the Eastern Church has remained unchanged from the earliest times up to the present day. Babies are baptized, chrismated (anointed with oil) and become full communicants in one rite. However, in the West, during and since the medieval period, changes in the theology and practice of initiation have taken place. From the fourth century large numbers of people were baptized over large geographical areas and it became impractical for candidates to gather around the bishop at Easter for a single celebration of initiation. The solution was to allow presbyters to conduct the whole rite, performing the anointing with oils previously blessed by the bishop (Jones and Tovey, 2002).

Where dioceses were small, for instance like

Rome and southern Italy, the practice of initiation in one rite continued. There were, however, times when the bishop was not available and the presbyter would conduct the whole rite, but omitted the post-immersion ceremonies, namely the prayer for the Holy Spirit accompanied by the laying on of hands and the anointing. Later, when the bishop came to the church he performed these actions. As the time between the initiation ceremony and the visit of the bishop was likely to be relatively short it still felt as if the process was one rite.

In time, this practice of having two parts to the initiation service was imposed upon the whole of the Western Church. The second part of the service, administered by the bishop, became known as 'confirmation'. The length of time between the initiation service and confirmation however, gradually grew and the confirmation service waned in significance. As it was a short service that seemed to add nothing to the original rite of initiation people saw little point in bringing their children to a second service. To encourage parents to do so, thirteenth century councils fixed upper age limits by which time children should have been confirmed. Over time the maximum age limits came to be thought of as the normal minimum age for confirmation; by the end of the Middle Ages it was generally considered inappropriate for the rite to be administered before the child was seven years old.

Paul and Maggie do not have experience of the rite of confirmation by a bishop. When they were baptized they made their own promises and were confirmed and received into membership of their churches immediately. Paul was baptized as a Methodist, during a public act of worship with Holy Communion. Beth remembers her confirmation, having to wear a white veil and the bishop laying his hands on her head. This rite took place when she was aged 13.

TO DO

What is your experience of confirmation?

Does it reflect confirmation as described in the Middle Ages?

Does confirmation have a role in today's Church?

Maggie, who believes strongly in adult baptism, is amazed to discover that by the end of the Middle Ages, infants were baptized within eight days of birth. They might then be confirmed after reaching the age of seven, also in a private ceremony, if they 'came across a bishop'. At this age they could receive communion, whether confirmed or not. The paschal character of initiation and its unity had disappeared by the end of the Middle Ages. Dipping the infant in water died out too, and the pouring of water over the baby became the norm (White, 2000).

At the Reformation new revised and simplified rites were drawn up. Although infant baptism was not questioned by the majority of the reformers, they insisted that it be made a public ceremony and in the vernacular. They removed most of the rites traditionally associated with Christian initiation, believing that these had either ceased to be understood or had come to be interpreted superstitiously.

Luther's baptismal rite of 1526 began at the church door, where the child's forehead was marked with the sign of the cross. This was followed with two prayers and an exorcism. There was a very keen sense of the presence of evil and evil forces, and exorcism was a series of intense prayers to rid the person of evil, so allowing the Holy Spirit to fill the candidate. Then came the reading from Mark 10.13–16, followed by the laying on of hands and the Lord's Prayer. People then moved to the font where the godparents made a triple renunciation and a triple profession of faith in the name of the child. The child was baptized and then robed in a white christening garment and blessed. Part of Beth's baptism was being robed in a white garment after she was immersed in water three times.

Some reformers instituted long speeches and addressed the godparents about their faith, as they could not be understood by the infant. In the section on baptism in the church order from Cologne commonly known as Hermann's *Consultation,* part of which was written by the reformer Martin Bucer, there was a public 'catechism' of the parents and godparents which took place on the Saturday evening prior to the baptism on Sunday (Jasper and Bradshaw, 1992). The catechism consisted of a very lengthy statement giving the true meaning of baptism, read by the minister. Following this the godparents were asked a long series of questions about their faith. After a further appeal to the godparents came the exorcism of the child, the making of the sign of the cross, two prayers, the reading of Mark 10.13–16, and an imposition of hands on the child, while the Lord's Prayer and creed were recited. The service ended with the recitation of certain psalms, and a prayer of thanksgiving along with a petition for the gift of the Holy Spirit. The child was then baptized the following day in the context of the Eucharist (Jones and Tovey, 2002).

In the Church of England *The Book of Common Prayer* of 1549 and 1552 insisted that baptism be administered on 'Sundays and Holy Days, when the most number of people may come together' (Cummings, 2013). *The Book of Common Prayer* 1549 was based on the Sarum baptismal rite and also Luther's rite and Hermann's *Consultation*. Public baptism began at the church door with an exhortation, and prayer for the candidate, based on Hermann. The godparents were asked the name of the child, and the priest made the sign of the cross on the candidate's head and breast. After further prayer, and an exorcism drawn from the medieval rite, the priest read Mark 10.13–16. Another exhortation based on the Mark reading followed, then came the Lord's Prayer and the creed, and final prayer, from Hermann. The baptismal party then moved into the church and to the font.

At the font, the priest emphasized to the godparents their responsibilities, making it clear that the baptismal promises would be made by the child through the godparents. A triple renunciation and triple profession of faith using the Apostles' Creed followed, then a form of blessing over the water, and the child was baptized with a triple immersion using the traditional formula. The service ended with a charge to godparents to inform the child of the solemn promises that had been made, and to bring the child for confirmation at the appropriate time.

The confirmation service was conservative. The major innovation was the catechism, which every child had to learn by heart before confirmation. After the prayer for the gifts of the Holy Spirit, the bishop would administer the sign of the cross and the laying on of hands. No oil was used. The rite ended with the peace, a concluding prayer based on Hermann, and the blessing.

The baptismal liturgy was changed in *The Book of Common Prayer* (1552) following criticism from

Martin Bucer. The service now began at the font instead of the church door, and the exorcism and other 'superstitious' sections were removed. The only ceremonial acts that remained were the baptism and the signing of the cross. The signing of the cross and the Lord's Prayer moved from before to after the baptism. There was no blessing of the water. The triple renunciation and profession of faith were run together, so that each was in the form of a single question addressed to the godparents.

Confirmation also changed and now the candidates were asked to 'ratify and confirm' what their godparents promised for them at baptism. The prayer for the sevenfold gifts of the Holy Spirit now asked that the Holy Ghost strengthen the candidate. The signing with the cross and the peace were also omitted (Jasper and Bradshaw, 1992).

In *The Book of Common Prayer* 1662 an order of adult baptism appeared for the first time. This was done partly to allow those not baptized as babies during the Civil War and during the Commonwealth to be baptized as adults. It also allowed the baptism of those being converted in the mission areas of the Church. The service for infant baptism remained substantially unchanged. The signing of the cross on the forehead of the baby remained despite the request of the Puritans for it to be removed. The confirmation service also remained substantially unchanged.

> **TO DO**
>
> Look at the baptism liturgy in *The Book of Common Prayer* 1662.
>
> How does it differ from today's baptism liturgy? What shift has there been in terms of the questions asked to godparents and the change of theological emphasis?

In the 1928 proposed revision of *The Book of Common Prayer* a few minor changes were made to the baptism service, including the following: parents were allowed to be godparents; deacons were permitted to baptize in the absence of the priest; and 'in the name of the child' was added to all the questions to be answered by godparents (Jasper and Bradshaw, 1992). The confirmation service changed theologically, with the renewal of baptism vows now consisting of a renunciation, an affirmation of faith, and a promise of lifelong obedience. The preface to this service suggested that 'a special gift of the Holy Spirit is bestowed through the laying on of hands with prayer'.

The Alternative Service Book 1980, following a number of reports on baptism, saw complete Christian initiation expressed in the rite of baptism, confirmation and Eucharist. In the infant baptism liturgy questions addressed to parents and godparents were answered 'for yourself and for this child'. This changed the understanding in *The Book of Common Prayer* of godparents speaking in the name of the child.

Other changes included the renaming of renunciation as 'the decision', which consisted of three short questions followed by the signing with the cross. There was a prayer for the blessing of the water and the declaration of faith took the form of three short questions. The use of oil in baptism and confirmation was permitted. The new confirmation service in *The Alternative Service Book 1980* was viewed as rather vague; as many saw initiation as complete in baptism, confirmation lost its distinctive identity.

As Paul, Beth and Maggie reflect on the development of baptism they are surprised how much emphasis was put on the notion of evil and how the vows undertaken have moved from parent and godparent to child and back again

The structure

Paul, Beth and Maggie are used to baptism being conducted in a modern format, as in *Common Worship*. The initiation services in *Common Worship* were published two years before the main volume of *Common Worship*. Beth notes the detailed introduction to the service of Christian initiation in *Common Worship* and the setting out of the theological and liturgical principles that underlie the initiation services. What is clear from this introduction is an understanding that baptism is the 'centrepiece around which the rites of confirmation, affirmation of baptismal faith and reception into the communion of the Church of England are clustered' (Jones and Tovey, 2002, p. 161). The initiation service of *Common Worship* is seen as a journey and the biblical language within the service reflects this understanding (Earey and Myers, 2001).

The development of the liturgy of Christian initiation was influenced by the report *On the Way* (Church of England, 1995), while being based on the baptismal practice of the Early Church as reflected in *The Book of Common Prayer*. All the initiation services are modelled on the modern Western eucharistic shape, whether or not the Eucharist is celebrated. The service begins with the preparation, which includes the greeting, the introduction and the collect. A trinitarian greeting introduces the preparation and may be followed by informal words of welcome.

The grace of our Lord Jesus Christ,
the love of God
and the fellowship of the Holy Spirit
be with you all
and also with you.

Prayer of thanksgiving

God our Creator,
we thank you for the wonder of new life
and for the mystery of human love.
We give thanks for all whose support and skill
surround and sustain the beginning of life.
As Jesus knew love and discipline within a human
   family,
may *these children* grow in strength and wisdom.
As Mary knew the joys and pains of motherhood,
give *these parents* your sustaining grace and love;
through Jesus Christ our Lord.
Amen.

(*Common Worship: Pastoral Services*, 2011)

The greeting may also include a prayer of
thanksgiving for the child before the president offers
the words of introduction.

Our Lord Jesus Christ has told us
that to enter the kingdom of heaven
we must be born again of water and the Spirit,
and has given us baptism as the sign and seal of
   this new birth.
Here we are washed by the Holy Spirit and made
   clean.
Here we are clothed with Christ,
dying to sin that we may live his risen life.

As children of God, we have a new dignity
and God calls us to fullness of life.
(*Common Worship: Pastoral Services*, 2011)

The *Gloria* may be used or the president moves to the collect of the day.

The liturgy of the word follows and this is almost identical in structure to the eucharistic rite. A choice is given of one or two readings before the Gospel and the wording 'may' be read is used rather than 'should' be read. As with the collect, the Sunday readings should be read, but there are alternative readings where 'baptism is the predominant element in the service' (Jones and Tovey, 2002). In the *Common Worship* initiation service a sermon is mandatory. Maggie had wondered why the last baptism she attended had included a sermon.

The presentation of the candidates follows and those who are old enough to speak for themselves are invited to affirm their wish to be baptized. When candidates speak for themselves the congregation is then asked to welcome and uphold them in their new life. For those who cannot speak for themselves, parents and godparents are required to commit to praying for the children and to supporting them in their journey of faith.

Having established the congregational support, the candidates or the parents and godparents now make their decisions to reject evil and to turn to Christ. The decision follows the ancient Eastern tradition of renunciation and adherence to Christ. The questions are set out in two blocks of three, and the parents and godparents are speaking for the children, unlike previously when they spoke for themselves.

The language of the questions is much stronger than in the three questions in *The Alternative Service Book 1980*, and a different verb is used in each question: reject, renounce, repent, turn, submit, come. The candidates receive the sign of the cross and this comes as a ritual response to the decision made by the candidates. Since they have committed themselves to follow Christ and to repent of their sins, the Church marks them with the cross as a symbol of God's acceptance of their decision.

The minister and candidates gather at the font for the prayer over the water. This is the central prayer of the whole rite and expresses the theology of the sacrament. The prayer in *Common Worship* is based on the initiation services from Canada and New Zealand. The prayer begins by listing significant biblical events associated with water, creation, exodus and the baptism of Jesus. Then it gives thanks for the baptismal water in which the candidates are buried and rise with Christ and are born again by the Holy Spirit, before finally asking God to sanctify the water through the Holy Spirit so that the candidates may be cleansed from sin and born again (Jones and Tovey, 2002).

> Loving Father,
> we thank you for your servant Moses,
> who led your people through the waters of the
>   Red Sea
> to freedom in the Promised Land.
> We thank you for your Son Jesus,
> who has passed through the deep waters of death
> and opened for all the way of salvation.
> Now send your Spirit,
> that those who are washed in this water
> may die with Christ and rise with him,
> to find true freedom as your children,
> alive in Christ for ever.
> (*Common Worship: Pastoral Services*, 2011)

After the prayer over the water there follows the affirmation of faith. This is divided into three questions and is professed by the whole congregation, unlike in previous liturgies of initiation. The baptism begins with a question to the candidates to affirm their faith then they are baptized in the name of the Trinity, although the number of times water is poured over the candidate is not mentioned.

The candidates can be clothed in a white robe. After the baptism or clothing the prayer said by the president concludes this part of the rite. The final prayer looks to the future and the continuing journey with Christ. The oil of chrism can be used at this point to anoint the newly baptized as a sign that the candidate has been reborn and is a new creation.

The commission sets the duties of the parents and godparents. This commission, post baptism, follows the tradition of *The Book of Common Prayer* of 1549, 1552 and 1662. The commission is split into two parts. The first is used where the newly baptized cannot answer for themselves; the second asks those who can answer for themselves five questions. After the commission there are prayers of intercession and then the welcome and peace follow. If the Eucharist is not celebrated the baptism liturgy ends with the sending out which includes the blessing, the giving of a lighted candle, and the dismissal.

Since the publication of these services in *Common Worship* concerns have been raised about the inaccessibility of the text to those who do not attend church. In 2011 a motion from the Diocese of Liverpool went to the Church of England General Synod, which stated:

that this Synod request the House of Bishops to ask the Liturgical Commission to prepare material to supplement the *Common Worship* Initiation provision, including additional forms of the Decision, the Prayer over the Water and the Commission, expressed in accessible language. (Church of England Liturgical Commission 2014, p. 2)

The Liturgical Commission was asked to prepare additional texts for consideration. The texts went to the House of Bishops in May 2013, and after further amendments were made the House of Bishops agreed in December 2013 to issue them for experimental use. Since November 2017 alternative baptismal texts have been made available. Guidance for their use is offered through the Church of England's website.

Conclusion

This chapter has looked at Christian initiation. It began by exploring where the symbols within baptism come from and how the theology of baptism has developed through the centuries.

Further reading

Church of England, 1995, *On the Way: Towards an integrated approach to Christian Initiation,* GSMisc444, London: Church House Publishing.

Church of England Liturgical Commission, 2014, *Christian Initiation Additional texts in Accessible*

Language, GS1958. London: General Synod of the Church of England.

Jasper,R.C.D.and Bradshaw,P.F.,1992, *A Companion to the Alternative Service Book,* London: SPCK.

Jones, S. and Tovey, P., 2002, 'Christian Initiation' in P. Bradshaw (ed.), *Companion to Common Worship,* pp. 148-178, London: SPCK.

White, J. F., 2000, *Introducing Christian Worship,* Nashville, TN: Abingdon Press.

White, S.J.,1997, *Groundwork of Christian Worship,* Peterborough: Epworth Press

www.churchofengland.org/prayer-and-worship/worship-texts-and-resources/common-worship/baptism

5

Engaging through Weddings

Paul, Beth and Maggie are having a conversation about marriage services. Paul has limited experience of marriage services. When his sister was married in a Methodist church they had a minister present, and also a marriage registrar. Beth has attended a number of weddings of friends and family in Anglican churches where the priest acts as registrar. Maggie reflects on her experience of both Anglican marriage services and Baptist marriage services.

As Paul, Beth and Maggie reflect together they ask the question: 'Is marriage Christian?' They recognize that some kind of pair-bonding ritual is very much part of the culture of societies across the world. In the United Kingdom a marriage ceremony has always been a formal occasion when a solemn, legal contract is made between a man and a woman (*The Methodist Worship Book*, 1999). While Paul, Beth and Maggie recognize the definition of a contract between a man and a woman, they are also aware that marriage is now entering a different understanding; but they assume that what is important is the legal contract between two people.

Lloyd (2013) suggests that in order to have a marriage 'you need two people who agree to commit themselves to one another, and the ratification of that brings with it an element of celebration, joy, thanksgiving, and blessing' (p. 168). The celebration, joy, thanksgiving and blessing come from the public recognition of their commitment through a public service with the community gathered around them.

Perham (2000) in his *New Handbook of Pastoral Liturgy* suggests that it is the bride and bridegroom who are the 'ministers of the sacrament'. The priest or deacon acts as the chief witness and as the registrar, in the Anglican context in England and Wales.

Paul, Beth and Maggie begin to look at the marriage service and the symbolism it contains. They reflect upon the giving and receiving of rings, the vows and promises made, and the blessing offered by the church through the minister. They begin their exploration, however, by looking at marriage in the Bible before moving on to look at the different marriage liturgies developed through the centuries.

The Bible and marriage

The Jewish Scriptures say little about marriage customs and nothing about wedding ceremonies. It is difficult to identify the precise details of wedding ceremonies in the Old Testament, perhaps because marriage was a civil contract. The Old Testament stories of the patriarchs describe lengthy episodes in their lives and these stories are woven with marriage and family ties. In the early Old Testament, the marriage norm is polygamy (one man marrying more than one wife), but the post-exilic prophets developed a high theology of marriage as being lifelong union of one man and one woman.

TO DO

Reflect on two marriage services you have attended. If you have experience of two different marriage services, for example a civil wedding and a church wedding, use these experiences to think about the differences and similarities between the two. Note how the ceremony is structured and what you think is going on at particular points in the ceremony.

There are hints about how marriage took place in the Jewish Scriptures; what is known is that there were two parts to marriage. First there was the betrothal, when the dowry was paid to the father of the bride, sometimes as a cash payment or sometimes in the form of goods. This payment was meant to bring security for the bride, and after the betrothal both parties had to adhere to the same restrictions as if they were husband and wife. Then the marriage itself consisted of two processions. The first was when the bridegroom and his friends went to collect the bride from her home. The second was the procession of the bride and groom to their future home. After this came the wedding banquet, ending with the bride being escorted by friends to the nuptial chamber (Earey and Myers, 2001).

In the Jewish Scriptures marriage was a duty and divorce was unacceptable. A woman was seen as a possession; she had no legal rights and could not divorce her husband for any reason. The husband, on the other hand, could divorce his wife and was not bound by any restrictions. All the husband had to do was hand the bill of divorcement to the wife in the presence of two witnesses.

In the New Testament there are a few stories, like the wise and foolish virgins and the wedding feast at Cana, that confirm the marriage customs of the Old Testament; other discussions around marriage in the New Testament are about ethical teaching rather than descriptions of marriage ceremonies. The instruction about marriage given in Matthew (19.5) emphasized the Genesis teaching about a man leaving his father and mother and the two becoming one flesh. St Paul in his letter to the Corinthians (1 Corinthians 7.39) speaks about Christian marriage being in 'the Lord'.

Maggie thinks about the whole idea of marriage and the notion of fidelity. She reflects on the society in which she lives and the number of friends she has seen get married who are now divorced. She thinks about the joy of the Christian community that came together to support her best friend in her marriage and the sadness when the marriage failed. She also considers the role of the church in marriage and the legal requirements for marriage, and wonders it would be better if these were separated.

TO DO

Write down some of the issues that face you as you think about marriage in today's society.

Is marriage good for society? Why do so many marriages fail?

History of marriage

The Church Fathers give some hints to the early Christian understanding of marriage. Ignatius of Antioch (AD *c*.107), writing to Polycarp, Bishop of Smyrna, insists on the sanctity of marriage and encourages the ceremony to take place with the permission and blessing of the bishop. Tertullian (an early Christian writer from Carthage in Africa) speaks of the relationship between man and woman as God-given, and wants the ceremony to be within the Eucharist with the blessing of the Church. Gregory of Nazianzus, fourth-century Bishop of Constantinople, talks about the joining of the right hands. Ambrose, Bishop of Milan in the fourth century, speaks of the veil and the benediction.

It is not until AD 866 that we find a full description of marriage, given by Pope Nicholas to the Bulgarians. Pope Nicholas speaks about three distinctive elements within the service: the espousal, the giving of a ring in the presence of witnesses, and the Mass following the ceremony.

As marriage developed in the West there were both religious and secular ceremonies. The religious rite was associated with the Eucharist, and included promises, prayers, exchange of rings and the drinking from a common cup by the bride and groom. The secular rites were built upon Roman paganism, where legally binding contracts were entered into by the parents of the couple and a soothsayer was consulted to determine the date of the marriage. On the day of the wedding the woman, dressed in yellow or orange fabric, was taken by a number of female attendants to the courtyard of the groom's house. There money was exchanged, and the groom gave a ring and placed it on the bride's fourth finger to signify that he owned her. The bride's parents offered corn to Zeus, asking that he would oversee the ceremony. A banquet followed and fertility symbols, especially walnuts, were thrown around the couple (White, 1997).

The marriage liturgy in the early medieval Church was not obligatory. Following the breakdown of social order in the seventh and eighth centuries, however, the Church felt it necessary to look at matrimonial consent and the conditions attached to it. To protect freedom of consent and to prevent deception, the rite of marriage in church developed in the twelfth century. At the doors of the church, the minister addressed the couple and asked about their consent. The bride was 'given away', the dowry was disclosed, and the ring was blessed and put on the right hand of the bride. The bridegroom gave pieces of gold or silver (according to his wealth) and the priest concluded the rite with his blessing. If a wedding Mass was to take place the couple and their families entered the church carrying candles. They made an offering at the offertory, the nuptial blessing was recited and the veil was laid on the head of the bride and on the shoulders of the bridegroom (Crichton, 1991).

As Beth reflects with Paul, and Maggie they talk about the symbols of marriage. The 'giving away' in particular makes them think about the notion of the woman being a possession of the man of the household, whether that be father or husband. They continue to reflect on the role of women historically and how still today women face issues of inequality. They go on to talk about the giving and receiving of rings as a symbol of love and commitment and a reminder of the promises the couple have made to each other.

> **TO DO**
>
> What are the symbols in the marriage service?
> Are they necessary? Why do you think they are
> important?

At the Reformation, the continental reformers detached marriage from the Eucharist but continued the customs and ceremonies that were already locally performed. Luther's rite had the couple give their consent at the church door, and then they were to exchange unblessed rings. The pastor joined their right hands using the words from Matthew 19.6 and pronounced them to be married. A procession moved into the church, where Scripture was read, and finally the pastor blessed the couple.

In Calvin's rite, marriage took place during the normal church worship, but not when the Eucharist was celebrated. After an address about the origin and purpose of marriage, the minister asked if there were any impediments. A prayer was said for the couple and then the couple was asked whether they consented and pledged themselves to each other. The pastor then said another prayer for the gift of the Spirit for the couple, read Matthew 19.3–6, pronounced that God had joined them together, and finished with a long prayer and a short blessing (Everett, 2006).

In Britain, the whole of the country was viewed as Christian and the only form of marriage allowed was the rite in *The Book of Common Prayer*. According to Cuming (1991), the marriage service in *The Book of Common Prayer* is close to its medieval predecessor. The 1549, 1552 and 1662 marriage services all began with a long address, expanded from the medieval 'banns', speaking of the institution of Christian marriage and the reasons for it, including children, continence (self-restraint) and company. For the first time in 1500 years in England the full wedding service took place inside the church.

Cranmer's rite of 1549 drew on the Sarum and Reformed rites to produce its shape. The service was divided into two parts. The first part, at the church door, began with the priest giving a long address and ended with the opportunity for any impediment to be voiced. The couple were also asked if there was any impediment to their marriage, and whether they consented to the marriage, in a form that combined the Luther and the Sarum rite. The giving away followed, with the priest asking, 'Who giveth this woman ...' The couple then joined hands and exchanged vows. The ring was given, unblessed, with the words 'With this ring ...' The couple then knelt, and the priest prayed over them; they joined hands and the priest read Matthew 19.6 and declared them to be married. A blessing of the couple based on the Sarum blessing concluded the first part of the service. During the recitation of the psalm the couple moved to the altar where prayers were said and then the Eucharist followed (Everett, 2006).

The 1552, 1559 and 1604 rites changed little from the 1549 (Cummings, 2013) despite Puritan opposition to the ring. The 1662 rite saw few alterations, even though a large amount of negotiation had taken place. What did change related to the Eucharist: now it was not 'normal' to follow the marriage with a Eucharist (Everett, 2006).

The theology of the marriage service of 1552, 1549 and 1662 emphasized 'lifelong' fidelity, with the assumption of the man being in charge as head of the household. The reasons given for marriage were for the procreation of children, sexual union and for the 'mutual society, help and comfort that the one ought to have of the other' (Cummings, 2013). Another assumption was that 'sexual union itself was a kind of concession allowed to the weakness of human nature, rather than an integral and joyful feature of the two becoming one' (Buchanan, Lloyd and Miller, 1980, p. 189).

The assumptions underlying Paul's understanding of marriage were becoming clearer as he talked with Beth and Maggie. He had often wondered why his parents always spoke of marriage being lifelong and why it felt to him as if their understanding of bringing children into the world had to be set in the context of marriage. He was also clearer now why marriage had been so important to them as a couple.

TO DO

Look at the understanding of the 'causes for which matrimony was ordained' as set out in *The Book of Common Prayer*. What order would you put them in?

Would you add any others? Or omit any?

The 1662 order of marriage was the only authorized marriage service in the Church of England until the twentieth century. The 1928 proposed revisions suggested changes reflecting the changing perception of marriage.

The *Alternative Services: Series One* marriage service was based on the 1928 service with the addition of the blessing of the ring. It differed from the *The Book of Common Prayer* 1662 marriage service in three ways (Cummings, 2013). First, the 'causes for which matrimony was ordained' were reworded. Second, an alternative form of vows was given whereby the couple could make the same promises to each other: 'to love and to cherish till death us do part'. The bride was no longer required to 'obey' her husband, though there was an option to do so, and the groom, instead of being required to endow his wife with all his worldly goods, was to share them with her. Third, the Eucharist could follow the marriage ceremony.

The marriage service was next amended in 1975 with the modern language of *Series Three*. It was authorized in 1977 and incorporated into *The Alternative Service Book 1980,* where it was suggested that marriage was to be celebrated within, rather than before, the Eucharist. Readings were an integral part of the service whether they came at the beginning of the service or before the prayers at the end. There was a liturgical greeting at the start of the service, and a modern form of the 1928 collect followed the preface, which remained traditional. The reasons for marriage were reordered, becoming mutual comfort, sexual union and children. The liturgy of *The Alternative Service Book 1980* moved to an understanding of the equal status of women and men. There were two sets of vows, and in the first set the couple made identical promises. After the vows the ring or rings were blessed with a simple and direct prayer that God would use the ring as a symbol to remind the couple of the promises they were making to one another. The rings became a sign of the relationship into which they had entered. The mutuality of the service was strengthened by the fact that both the man and the woman made a statement in the giving and receiving of the rings.

Maggie, as she thinks about the giving and receiving of rings, now understands more fully the upset of her mother when she lost her wedding ring. She wanted to have her new ring blessed, and even went further in renewing her wedding vows.

In *The Alternative Service Book 1980* no form of words were printed for 'giving away' the bride. This further reflected the change in society and the equality of men and women. The service also offered the couple a greater choice of Bible readings and prayers (Earey, Gay and Horton, 2001).

Finally, it also made it clear that the couple, not the priest, were the ministers of the sacrament. They were marrying each other and the role of the priest was to pronounce the Church's blessing on the couple.

Paul thinks that the role of the minister is clearer in the marriage service of the Methodist Church. He tells Beth and Maggie that in the introduction to *The Methodist Worship Book* (1999) it clearly states: 'A marriage ceremony is a formal occasion when a solemn, legal contract is made between a man and a woman' (p. 367). Paul also says that it is clear in the notes of the worship book that 'an authorised person (or the registrar) and two witnesses' need to hear the words of declaration and the words of contract. In an Anglican church, Beth informs them, the priest acts as the registrar, so it can easily confuse people into thinking that the priest is marrying the couple rather than giving the Church's blessing. Maggie's experience of marriage has been that it is not a sacrament of the Church, but nonetheless she would want to see people marry in church.

As Paul, Beth and Maggie begin to reflect on the newest of the marriage liturgies in *Common Worship* they see that the emphasis there is on marriage as a gift and blessing from God, rather than a legal contract.

The structure

Beth is familiar with the marriage service from *Common Worship*. She has attended a number of weddings over the past few years and talks about the structure of the marriage service. In her church they produce orders of service for people to follow, and one of the key pieces of information in the service booklet is the pastoral introduction. She feels that it is key because it clearly sets out the Christian understanding of marriage. In the pastoral introduction a wedding is described as 'one of life's great moments, a time of solemn commitment as well as good wishes, feasting and joy'. Marriage is spoken of as 'a creative relationship as (God's) blessing enables husband and wife to love and support each other …'

Paul recognizes the Methodist service of marriage in the structure of the *Common Worship* service. While the headings marking the various parts of the liturgy are different, the content is remarkably similar.

As Beth reflects on the marriage liturgy itself, she notices that it is split into two parts, the introduction and the marriage. The introduction part of the service prepares the couple and the congregation for the commitment of marriage. The preface tells people what marriage is about.

> In the presence of God, Father, Son and Holy Spirit,
> we have come together
> to witness the marriage of N and N,
> to pray for God's blessing on them,
> to share their joy
> and to celebrate their love.
> Marriage is a gift of God in creation
> through which husband and wife may know the grace of God.
> It is given
> that as man and woman grow together in love and trust,
> they shall be united with one another in heart, body and mind,
> as Christ is united with his bride, the Church.
> The gift of marriage brings husband and wife together
> in the delight and tenderness of sexual union
> and joyful commitment to the end of their lives.
> It is given as the foundation of family life
> in which children are [born and] nurtured
> and in which each member of the family,

in good times and in bad,
may find strength, companionship and comfort,
and grow to maturity in love.
Marriage is a way of life made holy by God,
and blessed by the presence of our Lord Jesus
  Christ
with those celebrating a wedding at Cana in
  Galilee.
Marriage is a sign of unity and loyalty
which all should uphold and honour.
It enriches society and strengthens community.
No one should enter into it lightly or selfishly
but reverently and responsibly in the sight of
  almighty God.
N and *N* are now to enter this way of life.
They will each give their consent to the other
and make solemn vows,
and in token of this they will [each] give and
  receive a ring.
We pray with them that the Holy Spirit will guide
  and strengthen them,
that they may fulfil God's purposes
for the whole of their earthly life together.
(*Common Worship: Pastoral Services*, 2011)

Then follows the declaration. The purpose of
the declaration is to ensure that the persons about
to marry are legally free to enter into the marriage

contract, that they wish to marry each other, and that they have the support of their families and friends. The declarations are normally followed by the collect, readings and sermon.

The part of the service headed Marriage contains the vows, the giving of rings, the proclamation (that they are married), the blessing of the marriage, the prayers, and the blessing of the congregation.

The Vows

The minister introduces the vows in these or similar words

N and N, I now invite you to join hands and make your vows,
in the presence of God and his people.

I, N, take you, N,
to be my wife,
to have and to hold
from this day forward;
for better, for worse,
for richer, for poorer,
in sickness and in health,
to love and to cherish,
till death us do part;
according to God's holy law.
In the presence of God I make this vow.

I, *N*, take you, *N*,
to be my husband,
to have and to hold
from this day forward;
for better, for worse,
for richer, for poorer,
in sickness and in health,
to love and to cherish,
till death us do part;
according to God's holy law.
In the presence of God I make this vow.

The Giving of Rings

Heavenly Father, by your blessing
let *these rings* be to *N* and *N*
a symbol of unending love and faithfulness,
to remind them of the vow and covenant
which they have made this day
through Jesus Christ our Lord.
All **Amen.**

N, I give you this ring
as a sign of our marriage.
With my body I honour you,
all that I am I give to you,
and all that I have I share with you,
within the love of God,
Father, Son and Holy Spirit.

N, I give you this ring
as a sign of our marriage.
With my body I honour you,
all that I am I give to you,
and all that I have I share with you,
within the love of God,
Father, Son and Holy Spirit.

*If only one ring is used, before they loose hands the
bride says*
N, I receive this ring
as a sign of our marriage.
With my body I honour you,
all that I am I give to you,
and all that I have I share with you,
within the love of God,
Father, Son and Holy Spirit.

The Proclamation

In the presence of God, and before this
congregation,
N and *N* have given their consent
and made their marriage vows to each other.
They have declared their marriage by the joining
of hands
and by the giving and receiving of *rings*.
I therefore proclaim that they are husband and
wife.

Those whom God has joined together let no one
put asunder.
(*Common Worship: Pastoral Services*, 2011)

What all three of them notice is that the historic
notion of betrothal, which in the Sarum rite took
place at the church door, has been put back into the
liturgy, and the consent has been separated from
the vows. They are also aware that the bride can
say her declaration before the groom and that the
parents can have a different role from that of 'giving
away'. The notes to the *Common Worship* marriage
service offer the opportunity for someone other
than the bride's father to present her and uses the
words, 'who brings this woman to be married to this
man'. Alternatively, the parents of the couple can
demonstrate their support when the minister says:

N and N have declared their intention towards
each other. As their parents will you entrust your
son and daughter to one another as they come to
be married?
Both sets of parents respond 'We will.'

There is also a congregational pledge of support.
Once the bride and groom have made their
declarations, the minister says:

Will you, the families and friends of N and N,

support and uphold them in their marriage now and in the years to come?

The congregation responds 'We will.'

The vows follow and are presented in simplified language while the substance is substantially the same as *The Alternative Service Book 1980,* and the giving of rings is unchanged. The norm now, however, is to exchange two rings. The proclamation pronounces them married and then the minister blesses the marriage. This nuptial blessing is a new composition. The prayers follow, ending with the Lord's Prayer. The dismissal is given. The signing of the register can take place either after the blessing of the marriage and before the prayers, or after the prayers. The aim of the clear structure and of the language in the *Common Worship* marriage service is to be 'user-friendly'. This is not, however, meant to detract from the solemnity of the occasion (Earey and Myers, 2001).

> **TO DO**
>
> Reflect on the questions offered to both the parents of the bride and groom and to the congregation. Are these useful additions? In what way do you think these two additions enhance the marriage service and what is the underlying message that they give?

Beth, Paul and Maggie recognize that, like other *Common Worship* liturgies, the marriage service does not stand alone, but is supported by other services and prayers. In *Common Worship*, as well as the marriage service itself there is a marriage service within the celebration of Holy Communion. Supplementary texts include prayers at the calling of the banns, an alternative preface, alternative readings, psalms and vows. There is a prayer at the giving of rings, and at the blessing of the marriage; and there are additional prayers and collects. There is also a liturgy for thanksgiving of marriage.

The wedding service within the context of a communion service has a fivefold structure: the gathering, the liturgy of the word, the marriage, the liturgy of the sacrament and the dismissal. The introduction parts of the wedding service are distributed between the gathering and the liturgy of the word.

Paul, Beth and Maggie realize that marriage is not just the one ceremony, it is a way of life. One of the strengths of the *Common Worship* marriage material is that it offers additional prayers and services to allow preparation for marriage and support the whole of married life, for example when banns are called. A service of 'Thanksgiving for Marriage' is given which can be adapted for a number of different occasions, including the renewal of marriage vows on an anniversary or at other times.

Paul, Beth and Maggie reflect that, although marriage was and is a legal arrangement, the Church has a key role to play in enabling couples to plan their wedding and their commitment to one another in a church context with the Church's blessing.

Conclusion

This chapter has explored the historical development of marriage within the Church. It has looked at the development of marriage in the history of the Church and the changing understanding of marriage from early Christian marriage services to marriage in the Church today.

Further reading

Bradshaw, P. (ed.), 2006, *Companion to Common Worship*, Vol 2, London: SPCK.

Earey, M.,Gay,P.and Horton, A.,2001, *Understanding Worship: A Praxis Study Guide*, London: Mowbray.

Earey, M. and Myers, G., 2001, *Common Worship Today: An illustrated guide to Common Worship*, London: Harper Collins.

White, J. F., 2000, *Introducing Christian Worship*, Nashville, TN: Abingdon Press.

www.churchofengland.org/prayer-and-worship/ worship-texts-and-resources/common-worship/ marriage

6

Engaging through Funerals

Paul, Beth and Maggie are having a conversation about death and about funerals in particular. Paul has limited experience of funerals as both sets of grandparents and his parents are still alive. Beth has more experience as her father recently died and her grandmother died a couple of years ago. Maggie also has experience of funerals with the death of her grandparents and of a sibling.

As they talk together they reflect on the purpose of a funeral. Beth says that for her the funeral of her dad was an opportunity to say goodbye and to reflect on her father's life. Maggie, on the other hand, sees the funeral as an opportunity not only to say goodbye, but also to proclaim the gospel message of Christ's death and resurrection. Paul listens to both Beth and Maggie and feels that whenever he has been to a funeral service he is aware that it is about commending the person to God, in so doing allowing the bereaved to leave the body and to say farewell.

Perham (2000) in *New Handbook of Pastoral Liturgy* suggests that a funeral seeks to bring a community together to do a number of things:

- to honour life;
- to commend the dead to God;
- to give space for grief and yet to move people on;
- to express the love and compassion of God to the bereaved;
- to proclaim the gospel message of Christ's death and resurrection;
- to warn of the inevitability of death and to encourage them to walk in this life with an eye to eternity;
- to take leave of the body and to say farewell;
- to dispose of the body reverently.
  (Perham, 2000, p. 195)

As Paul, Beth and Maggie continue to reflect on funerals, they realize that the nature of funerals has changed. In the past people gathered in the parish church or the local chapel, a building people would have attended regularly. The deceased would have been known in the community in which they lived and worked, and so the whole community would have come together to support the family and to say farewell.

As Paul, Beth and Maggie continue in conversation, they begin to look back into the history of the Church and how the dead have been taken care of. They look first at funerals and the Bible before moving on to the history of funerals in the Early Church.

The Bible and funerals

In the New Testament there are no descriptions of funerals, and Giles (2006) suggests that the early Christians would have adopted the practices of the Jewish tradition. For the Jews burying their dead was an important ritual because they believed that corpses were unclean and had to be disposed of as soon as possible. The burial of the dead was so important that it took precedence over any other religious obligation. The burial itself involved the reciting of the *Kaddish*, a prayer that talks of the coming of the kingdom and the hope of resurrection. Scripture was read from the book of Job or Psalm 16. Three days of weeping followed and four days without work; after this period came three weeks of official mourning (Giles, 2006). There was nearly always a funeral meal at home after the Jewish burials. Rites of purification followed, and until these had been completed mourners were not allowed to carry out any other religious duties.

In the New Testament writings there are tiny clues to early Christian funeral practice. The Gospels refer to the burial of Jesus (Mark 15.42–47) and of Lazarus (John 11.1–44) and these reveal something of the way Jewish people prepared the bodies of the dead for burial. Another story, the raising to life of the widow of Nain's son, shows how a crowd of mourners were processing to the place of burial (Luke 7.11–17).

Earey, Gay and Horton (2001) suggest that there are further references in later Christian texts that demonstrate a strong sense of resurrection hope and that funeral ceremonies began at home. Prayers would have been said as the body was ceremonially washed, anointed and wrapped in white linen. The body was then carried to the cemetery, which was outside the city walls, while the mourners sang psalms of hope and praise. People wore white, and carried palm leaves and lights. At the graveside the community would have said prayers and celebrated the Eucharist.

The ancient Roman practice at this time began with various ceremonies in the home, including the preparation of the body. The funeral procession to the graveside took place at night. Everyone wore black and the burial or cremation was followed by a funeral feast at the graveside. After the funeral there were purification ceremonies for the relatives and also for the dead person's house (Earey, Gay and Horton, 2001).

> **TO DO**
>
> How does the Early Church reflect what happens today? What are the similarities and what are the differences?
>
> Who do you think a funeral is for? Note down the reasons for your answer.

History of funerals

The Apostolic Tradition cites the existence of Christian cemeteries and discusses the cost of funerals, which were to be kept reasonable. Tertullian (an early Christian writer from Carthage in Africa) indicates that there was a funeral Eucharist and an annual Eucharist on the anniversary of death. *The Sacramentary of Serapion* (a fourth-century liturgical tradition of the Church of Egypt) talks about prayer for a dead person before burial, and John Chrysostom (fourth-century Archbishop of Constantinople and Early Church Father) speaks of hymns and psalms being sung at funerals.

The earliest account of anything like a Christian funeral can be found in St Augustine's *Confessions* (Book IX) in which he describes the death of his mother Monica.

So when the body was carried forth, we both

went and returned without tears. For neither in those prayers we poured forth to thee, when the sacrifice of our redemption was offered up to thee for her – with the body placed by the side of the grave as is the custom there, before it is lowered down into it – neither in those prayers did I weep. (White, 1997, p. 167)

At this time there were different practices but a common pattern for funerals. The funeral began at the house. Introductory prayers and responses were said and psalms were said or sung. Then followed a procession either to the church or to the tomb while psalms were chanted and palm leaves and lights were carried. At the tomb there was a service consisting of prayers, hymns, psalms and readings. The final 'kiss of peace' was offered. The Eucharist was celebrated either in the church or at the graveside (Giles, 2006).

In the medieval Western Church the joy and triumph, the waving of palm branches and shouts of alleluia had gone and been replaced with penitential psalms, with people dressed in black; instead of confidence in the resurrection a deep consciousness of sin and judgement prevailed. Prayer for the dead was no longer joyful recognition of communion together in Christ, but a desperate pleading for release from punishment. Hell and purgatory became part of the religious understanding of death.

As a consequence the rich left money to the church so that masses might be said for their souls. Chantry chapels were built in churches to accommodate the increase in the number of masses.

Funerals became public events at which the Church attempted to discipline the people, while murals and altar paintings expressed the torments of the damned and the rewards of the faithful. The medieval liturgy for the office of the dead introduced a Latin anthem called *Dies irae,* which reflected the emphasis on damnation rather than the hope of salvation encouraged by the Early Church (Giles, 2006). At the Council of Trent in 1563, the doctrine of purgatory was reaffirmed and prayers for the dead commended.

By the end of the Middle Ages there was a shorter funeral liturgy. The prayers for the dying person and the funeral rite were separated. Now the liturgy began after death on arrival at the dead person's house with a psalm and a sentence of Scripture. The body was then carried to the church while a penitential psalm, Psalm 51 (*Miserere mei Deus*) was recited. The office of the dead, which included readings and psalms, was then said, followed by the funeral Mass, the sprinkling of the coffin with holy water and the absolution of the dead. An anthem and psalms were recited as the coffin was taken in procession to the grave, which was blessed before the body was laid in it. The graveside service ended with the *Kyrie* (Lord, have mercy), the Lord's Prayer, responses and a prayer for the dead person. The people then moved back to church and seven penitential psalms were said (Buchanan, Lloyd and Miller, 1980).

Paul, Beth and Maggie reflect on the funerals they have attended and the differences in these services. The differences were mainly because of the deceased person's Christian commitment or lack of it. As they think about the whole experience of death, Beth suddenly realizes that the prayers at the time of her father's death were part of the same liturgy that continues in the funeral service, at the crematorium and at the burial of the mortal remains. She, like Paul and Maggie, had always seen them as separate services.

TO DO

Christian burial ceremonies have always reflected the tension between mourning and celebration. In your experience, how have these tensions been expressed or resolved?

Have you attended a funeral service of real celebration and joy in the resurrection to eternal life? Or have you only experienced deep sadness?

At the Reformation the continental reformers wanted to simplify the rites of death and burial. One extreme example can be seen in the tradition of John Knox, a Scottish reformer, as later described in the *Westminster Directory* published by Parliament in 1645:

> When any person departeth this life, let the dead body on the day of burial, be decently attended from the house the place of burial, and there immediately be interred, without any ceremony. And because the customs of kneeling down, and praying by, or towards the dead corpse, and other such usages, in the place where it lies before it is carried to burial are superstitious: and for that praying, reading and singing both in going to, and at the grave have been grossly abused, are in no way beneficial to the dead, and have proved many ways hurtful to the living, therefore let all things be laid aside. (Buchanan, Lloyd and Miller, 1980, p. 213)

The reformers wanted to return a sense of hopefulness and joy to the funeral rite and belief in the resurrection. They particularly opposed the medieval Christian doctrine of purgatory, the belief that after death souls moved into an 'in-between' state during which they underwent a time of painful spiritual purgation in preparation for heaven. The reformers taught that the death and resurrection of Christ was sufficient for the salvation of Christian believers. They believed that once a person was dead they were subject to judgement and they could not be helped, nor could God be influenced by prayers for the dead.

Martin Luther understood the funeral to be for the living rather than the departed, offering the promise of eternal life. He urged the singing of joyful hymns. John Knox's Genevan Prayer Book of 1556 says that the body should be brought reverently to the grave, accompanied by mourners, but that a sermon should be preached in the church after the body had been buried (Giles, 2006).

Thomas Cranmer's *Book of Common Prayer* of 1549 supported the theology of the continental reformers and moved away from the medieval practice. He stipulated a procession to church, or to the grave, and as people processed scriptural sentences would be sung or said. Then the body was buried and during the burial more sentences and words of committal and commendation would be said, ending with earth thrown on to the body in the grave. After the interment, or sometimes before, a non-eucharistic service would be said in church, at which Psalms 116, 139 and 146 would be used, together with a reading from 1 Corinthians

15.20–58, and the *Kyrie*, the Lord's Prayer and the responses. A final prayer for the deceased would end the service. After this the Eucharist was celebrated (Giles, 2006).

A more radical revision came in 1552 when Cranmer omitted all singing of the psalms, the provision for Holy Communion and all prayers for the dead. The office consisted of a procession to the grave, the words of committal, and a concluding prayer and collect. The whole service, now much shortened, was carried out at the graveside.

The Book of Common Prayer 1662 changed very little of the funeral office. It added Psalms 39 and 90, to be used on arrival at church, and the reading from 1 Corinthians followed. A rubric denying Christian burial to those excommunicated, suicides, or the unbaptized was added.

The funeral rite of 1662 is directed at the living, not the dead, to provide both comfort and challenge in the face of death. It speaks clearly of resurrection and of hope, though its solemnity inhibits it from expressing the joy and praise of the earliest Christian funerals (Cummings, 2013).

Paul remembers attending the funeral service of an elderly friend of the family. He reflects on the decision of the deceased who wanted a 1662 funeral service; this was because John Wesley, in preparing a funeral service for Methodists in North America, followed almost exactly the rite of the burial of the dead in *The Book of Common Prayer* 1662. What Paul remembers is the language and order that the service brought, and how the resurrection of the dead was so evident in the words and hymns.

TO DO

Look at *The Book of Common Prayer* 1662 funeral office and compare it to the liturgy in *Common Worship* or that used in your own tradition.

What are the similarities?

What are the differences?

Which service do you prefer and why?

In 1928 major revisions to *The Book of Common Prayer* were proposed. The suggested revisions for the funeral service provided additional readings and prayers. Additional sentences were added to the opening procession and when the body was taken to the graveside the use of Psalm 103.13–17 was allowed instead of the traditional sentences. A new prayer of committal based on Cranmer's commendation from 1549 was offered as an alternative. The proposed revisions also gave an order for the funeral of a child, and mentioned the possibility of a memorial service, but gave no direction for cremation, which had become popular.

While the 1928 proposed revision of *The Book of*

Common Prayer was never officially authorized, some of the prayers appeared in *Alternative Services: Series One*. *Series Two* effectively concluded that there was one service for all baptized people including those who had taken their own lives. There was a separate service for children. *Series Two* failed to get assent in the House of Laity because of the inclusion of prayers for the dead. *Series Three* included material from both *Series Two* and the 1928 proposed revision, but changed the title of the service from Burial to Funeral Services.

The Alternative Service Book 1980 revised the provision of the opening sentences, and put the collect from the 1928 burial service into modern speech. Psalm 121 was added along with suggestions for alternatives. The reading from John 16.1–6 was also added. The traditional use of the whole of 1 Corinthians 15 changed and selected verses were included. Other suggested readings were included as alternatives. An optional sermon followed the readings. Verses from the *Te Deum* (an early hymn praising God the Trinity) were recommended, but many chose a hymn instead. The prayers in *The Alternative Service Book 1980* began with the Lesser Litany and Lord's Prayer. Prayers could now be offered that gave a freedom to pray for the dead if so desired. The commendation followed, which described the whole person ('our brother/sister') as having been entrusted to God. After this was the committal, which committed the person's body to earth or fire (Giles, 2006).

Within *The Alternative Service Book 1980* there was a child's funeral service, and a selection of prayers for the funeral of stillborn or newly born infants. A brief service for the interment of ashes was offered, based on the committal, as was a service for the laying of a body in a church prior to the funeral. Finally there was a funeral in the context of Holy Communion.

As Paul, Beth and Maggie reflect on these changes they comment on them in the light of a changing society. They recognize that twentieth-century worshippers have neither the excitement and hope of the early Christians nor the fear of hell and damnation of medieval Christians. They also recognize there is a reluctance for people to think and talk about death, even as part of the Christian message. They discuss the fact that funerals are not always conducted in a church, but increasingly take place in a cemetery or crematorium. Cremations have become the norm and death itself often happens out of the sight of other people in order to protect them from the reality of death. They recognize that this was the new reality and Maggie's experience of being with her sibling when she died was unusual.

As they consider the funeral liturgy in *The Alternative Service Book 1980* they realize that it was weak in acknowledging the feelings of fear, doubt and sorrow. It was also a liturgy aimed at those who attend church.

TO DO

What is your experience of death?

Did the death of a loved one happen away from the home in a hospital or hospice? Or did it happen in the home?

What are the positives and negatives of the funeral liturgy which includes prayers for the dying?

The structure

Paul, Beth and Maggie recognize a structure to the funeral services they have attended. Beth planned the funeral service for her father with her parish priest. The priest explained to her that while there were set parts of the service that had to be included there was a fair amount of flexibility within the service to include one of her father's favourite poems and music that he wanted. She also remembers the prayers at the time of his death.

Common Worship: Pastoral Services (Church of England, 2011) begins its pastoral office for funerals with Ministry at the Time of Death. The first part of the service offers a service of reconciliation to the dying person. The next part is for helping those who sit and watch beside the dying to come to terms with the inevitability and closeness of death.

The preparation precedes the ministry of reconciliation and is used with the dying person present. Short sentences begin the office, offering hope and comfort. Then follows the Lord's Prayer. The service moves into a service of reconciliation where the dying person may express some form of penitence, then absolution is offered. The liturgy offers the opportunity for a short confession or a longer one if the person is conscious.

When the ministry of reconciliation is complete the service moves into an opening prayer section with prayers at the time of death. Included within this part of the service is the opportunity to read Scripture, to pray, to lay on hands and anoint, to receive Holy Communion, and to commend the person to God. At the time of death or shortly afterwards there are resources to pray for the dead person.

Common Worship: Pastoral Services (2011) offers a number of short services to be used before the funeral: prayers at home before the funeral, prayers for those unable to be present at the funeral, the reception of the coffin at church before the funeral, a funeral vigil, and prayers on the morning of the funeral.

The main funeral liturgy begins with a pastoral

introduction, which makes clear that every life is precious to God, and that there is hope and new life in Christ. The purpose of the funeral service according to the pastoral introduction is:

> To use this occasion to express our faith and our feelings as we say farewell, to acknowledge our loss and our sorrow, and to reflect on our own mortality. Those who mourn need support and consolation. (p. 256)

The funeral service in *Common Worship* suggests a structure that should include the gathering, readings and sermon, prayers, commendation and farewell, the committal, and the dismissal. Within this structure is scope for flexibility. At the gathering, the traditional sentences of Scripture are read. There is also the opportunity to use a pall, the sprinkling of baptismal water and symbols of the deceased person's life.

In the introduction, further words of explanation are offered, followed by a prayer that focuses on the grief of the congregation. There is a choice of two prayers and *Common Worship* draws on *Celebrating Common Prayer* (1992) and the *New Zealand Prayer Book* (1989).

God of all consolation,
your Son Jesus Christ was moved to tears
at the grave of Lazarus his friend.

Look with compassion on your children in their
loss;
give to troubled hearts the light of hope
and strengthen in us the gift of faith,
in Jesus Christ our Lord.   **Amen.**

or

 Almighty God,
you judge us with infinite mercy and justice
and love everything you have made.
In your mercy
turn the darkness of death into the dawn of new
life,
and the sorrow of parting into the joy of heaven;
through our Saviour, Jesus Christ. **Amen.**
(*Common Worship: Pastoral Services*, 2011)

A hymn may be sung followed by the tribute. An
addition to the funeral liturgy of *Common Worship*
are prayers of penitence, which are based on the
eucharistic prayers of penitence. The collect gathers
the prayers of the people together before moving
to the ministry of the word. In *Common Worship:
Pastoral Services* (2011) there must be a psalm or
hymn, a New Testament reading and a sermon.
Following the ministry of the word comes the
prayers, which may end with the Lord's Prayer.

The commendation and committal follow, the
distinction between the two remaining as suggested

in *Series Two*. The commendation begins with *The Alternative Service Book 1980* introductory sentence and silence is suggested. A prayer of 'entrusting and commending' is offered but there are others permitted. The prayer entrusts the whole person to God, creator and redeemer. It 'claims' the promises made in Christ, and talks about eternal life (Giles, 2006).

> Let us commend *N* to the mercy of God,
> our maker and redeemer.
>
> *Silence is kept.*
>
> God our creator and redeemer,
> by your power Christ conquered death
> and entered into glory.
> Confident of his victory
> and claiming his promises,
> we entrust *N* to your mercy
> in the name of Jesus our Lord,
> who died and is alive
> and reigns with you,
> now and for ever. **Amen.**
> (*Common Worship: Pastoral Services*, 2011)

The committal may begin with a sentence of Scripture, which leads into two texts, one from *The Book of*

Common Prayer 1662 and the other from *The Alternative Service Book 1980*. The first is Psalm 103.8, 13–17 and the second is a tenth-century anthem by Notker. Like the rest of the text, this has been written in modern, inclusive language (Giles, 2006).

Three committal prayers are provided for different contexts. The prayer for burial uses the familiar 'ashes to ashes' and keeps Cranmer's reference to the ground. The prayer for cremation speaks of a two-stage process. The body is 'given' to be cremated and handed back later for the ashes to be interred. If the ashes are not to be interred the whole of the third prayer below is used.

Either

The Lord is full of compassion and mercy,
slow to anger and of great goodness.
As a father is tender towards his children,
so is the Lord tender to those that fear him.
For he knows of what we are made;
he remembers that we are but dust.
Our days are like the grass;
we flourish like a flower of the field;
when the wind goes over it, it is gone
and its place will know it no more.
But the merciful goodness of the Lord endures for
ever and ever toward those that fear him
and his righteousness upon their children's
children.

Or

We have but a short time to live.
Like a flower we blossom and then wither;
like a shadow we flee and never stay.
In the midst of life we are in death;
to whom can we turn for help,
but to you, Lord, who are justly angered by our
sins?
Yet, Lord God most holy, Lord most mighty,
O holy and most merciful Saviour,
deliver us from the bitter pain of eternal death.
Lord, you know the secrets of our hearts;
hear our prayer, O God most mighty;
spare us, most worthy judge eternal;
at our last hour let us not fall from you,
O holy and merciful Saviour.

The minister uses one of the following forms of Committal.

At the burial of a body

We have entrusted our *brother/sister N* to God's
mercy,
and we now commit *his/her* body to the ground:
earth to earth, ashes to ashes, dust to dust:
in sure and certain hope of the resurrection to
eternal life
through our Lord Jesus Christ,

who will transform our frail bodies
that they may be conformed to his glorious body,
who died, was buried, and rose again for us.
To him be glory for ever. **Amen.**

*Or, in a crematorium, if the Committal is to follow at
the Burial of the Ashes*

We have entrusted our *brother/sister N* to God's
mercy,
and now, in preparation for burial,
we give *his/her* body to be cremated.
We look for the fullness of the resurrection
when Christ shall gather all his saints
to reign with him in glory for ever. **Amen.**

*Or, in a crematorium, if the Committal is to take place
then*

We have entrusted our *brother/sister N* to God's
mercy,
and we now commit *his/her* body to be cremated:
earth to earth, ashes to ashes, dust to dust:
in sure and certain hope of the resurrection to
eternal life
through our Lord Jesus Christ,
who will transform our frail bodies
that they may be conformed to his glorious body,

who died, was buried, and rose again for us.
To him be glory for ever. **Amen.**
(*Common Worship: Pastoral Services*, 2011)

The dismissal gives a clear ending to the service and includes the Lord's Prayer, if it has not been said earlier, the *Nunc dimittis* (also known as the Song of Simeon), three concluding prayers and an ending that may be a blessing if a priest is present.

Common Worship: Pastoral Services offers a funeral service within the context of a celebration of Holy Communion, and a funeral service for a child. It also gives the opportunity for services after the funeral that include prayers in the home. These prayers offer peace to the house, and the opening greetings speak of 'opening a door to a new life'. In addition it provides a service for the burial of ashes and gives guidance for memorial services.

Paul, Beth and Maggie, having spent time looking at the different funeral services, feel that the *Common Worship* service is the most sensitive to the pastoral context. What they recognize is that the *Common Worship* service is very personal. In *The Book of Common Prayer* 1662 the deceased was never mentioned by name. *Common Worship: Pastoral Services* (2000) like *The Alternative Service Book 1980* allows the deceased to be named in the prayers and additionally allows tributes to be made. There is great sensitivity to the needs of the congregation. People are welcomed to the service; family or friends may give tributes; and may also, with the consent of the officiating minister, place symbols of the deceased's life and faith on the coffin. The different prayers offered acknowledge the reality of people's grief and pray for them (Earey, Gay and Horton, 2001).

Conclusion

This chapter has explored the funeral rites from the beginning of Christianity to the present day. The chapter has discussed the changes that have taken place in the funeral liturgy as society has changed in its understanding of death.

Further reading

Bradshaw, P. (ed.), 2006, *Companion to Common Worship*, Vol 2, London: SPCK.

Earey, M., Gay, P. and Horton, A., 2001, *Understanding Worship: A Praxis Study Guide*, London: Mowbray.

White, J. F., 2000, *Introducing Christian Worship*, Nashville, TN: Abingdon Press.

White, S. J., 1997, *Groundwork of Christian Worship* Peterborough: Epworth Press.

www.churchofengland.org/prayer-and-worship/
worship-texts-and-resources/common-worship/
funerals

7

Music and Song

Paul, Beth and Maggie are having a conversation about hymns, music and worship songs. As a member of a Methodist church Paul has been brought up on the hymns of John and Charles Wesley. His church enjoys singing hymns. As a member of an Anglo-Catholic church Beth has experienced different forms of liturgical music through the singing of different eucharistic settings. As a member of an evangelical Anglican church Maggie has been brought up on worship songs, especially Graham Kendrick.

Paul, when studying at university, came into contact with the music of the Taizé community and enjoyed the meditative repetition of the singing of simple chants. Beth has experience of Gregorian chant and this comes from time spent staying at different monasteries. Maggie has recently been to Derby Cathedral and heard the choir sing Evensong, which included the singing of psalms, responses, canticles, hymns and an anthem. She comments that it was beautiful, but so different from what she is used to.

TO DO

What is your experience of music in worship?
Are hymns sung or worship songs?
Make a list of all the music that happens in
your regular act of worship.
Are there parts of the liturgy that are always
sung?

The Bible and music and song

In both the Old and New Testaments references are
made to psalms and hymns, though a search through
the New Testament for musical references will reveal
very few. Today, music is a discipline with a separate
existence, and singing is different from speaking. The
boundary between singing and speaking was far less
clear in the Early Church. In the Apostolic Church
there was a 'lyrical quality' in its liturgical assemblies
(Gelineau, 1992). This is evidenced in the canticles of
the opening chapters of Luke's Gospel, and in some
passages in Paul's writings.

The New Testament contains references to people
singing hymns and the advice for people to sing
hymns as praise to God. In the Acts of the Apostles
Paul and Silas spend the night in jail at Philippi
'praying and singing hymns to God' (Acts 16.25).
In the Epistle of James (5.13) this advice is given:

'Are any cheerful? They should sing songs of praise.' In Paul's writings there are positive instructions on the issue of singing in the Christian assembly, for example in Colossians 3.16, 'with gratitude in your hearts sing psalms, hymns and spiritual songs to God', and in Ephesians 5.19. According to Gelineau (1992), two characteristics of Christian singing emerge from the New Testament. First, singing must be filled with the Holy Spirit, and second, singing must be the expression of conscious faith. It is not a question of making music for its own sake, but of expressing the word of God.

The history of music and song

In writings from the first three centuries of the Church there are many references to singing at worship. There are also a number of hymn texts from that period. Pliny the younger, a Roman official who was governor of the province of Pontus and Bithynia in Asia Minor in AD 111 to 112, speaks of the practices of Christians singing a hymn (*carmen*) to God. During this period there is also evidence from Africa, Egypt and the East that the Church of the martyrs was rich in song.

In the second and third centuries there was a large amount of creativity in hymn writing. From Gnostic circles there is the Hymn to Jesus or the Hymn of the Soul. There is also the *Phos hilaron* (song of the light) and the earliest kernel of the *Gloria in excelsis* (Gelineau, 1992). The earliest hymns had a strongly Christological character. In form they avoided classical meters and remained close to the poetry of the Bible and to rhythmic prose.

By the time of Clement of Alexandria in the late second century a metrical structure began to emerge in which all the syllables had the same duration, known as the *isosyllabic tendency* of Christian hymnody. The words became more important than the poetry or music.

After Constantine, in the fourth and fifth centuries the psalms began to be sung responsorially throughout the whole of the Christian world. A cantor or soloist would sing the psalm, and the congregation would sing a refrain from the psalm between each verse.

Beth is aware of this type of psalm singing. In her church the psalm is sung in this way at the Eucharist. They have a cantor who sings the main verses of the psalm and the congregation responds with the refrain. She prefers this way of singing the psalm rather than the antiphonal way, which she has heard at Evensong.

> **TO DO**
> What is your experience of singing psalms in worship?
> Are psalms led by the choir?
> Are they said?
> Why do you think psalms are important in worship?

As the responsorial psalm developed in this period some variations emerged. In the fifth century the term antiphony was first used in the context of saying the psalms. The assembly would have been divided into two choirs or choruses, which in turn repeated the refrain. Gradually, non-biblical texts were used in the refrains. This form of saying the psalm later developed into what some call antiphonal psalmody, but is more accurately described as alternating psalmody, where the two halves of the community sang the verse alternately (Sinclair, 2002).

From the sixth century, congregational participation in the liturgy reduced and alongside this development the old responsorial psalmody lost its importance. In the West the refrain was no longer repeated after each verse. Gradually the verses came to be recited alternately by two choirs, and the whole psalm was preceded and concluded by an antiphon almost always taken from Scripture. Ecclesiastical singing eventually became the norm for monks and clergy only and the people were left to watch and listen (Gelineau, 1992).

In the Middle Ages, the developments in church music generally came from the monasteries. Monastic life revolved around singing public prayer eight times a day and included singing a night office. The services took place in the quire and this space was divided into two parallel sections of stalls, where the psalms would be sung responsorially. Dialogues were sung as responsories or invitatories; for example, 'O Lord, open our lips' followed by 'And our mouth shall show forth thy praise' (White, 2000).

The musical style that developed was Gregorian chant or plainsong. Gregorian chant is sung in unison rather than in harmony, so all voices are united in a single pitch. The music was communal as well as contemplative, allowing the words rather than the music to speak. Office hymns were written to add to the scriptural components, for various times of day and to commemorate special occasions. A late example of an office hymn is Bishop Thomas Ken's 'All praise to Thee, my God, this night' which ends with the doxology, 'Praise God, from whom all blessings flow'. Beth remembers this hymn from the time she attended a Lent study group. At the end of the session everyone sang this hymn from *Mission Praise*, although she had no idea of its roots in monasticism.

In the Middle Ages monastic forms of worship influenced daily public prayer for parochial use. They developed church music and also shaped church architecture. In the Eucharist or Mass there were six fixed musical texts: the *Kyrie* (Lord, have mercy), the *Gloria* (Glory be to God on high), the *Credo* (I believe), the *Sanctus* (Holy, holy, holy ...), the *Benedictus* (Blessed is he), and the *Agnus Dei* (Lamb of God).

The Propers (varying text) of the Mass changed to fit the lessons and seasons. These were the introit (the psalm at the beginning of the rite), the gradual (after the epistle), the alleluias (before the Gospel), the offertory and communion (usually a psalm verse before communion) (White, 2000). Most singing was done by choirs, unaccompanied and in Latin. It was not until the late nineteenth century that the pipe organ came into large parish churches.

By the eleventh century, an Italian monk, Guido D'Arezzo, had begun to develop what would now be termed a musical stave. He developed a way of putting on parallel lines signs that would now be recognised as notes, giving their pitch. Later came the development of defining the length of a note. In the late Middle Ages there developed multi-voice singing known as polyphony. Alongside the many voices there was the singing of different melodies and texts.

The Reformation in the sixteenth century

brought differences of opinion in the use of music in church services, ranging from the abolition of music to services being almost completely musical. The Council of Trent in the mid-sixteenth-century debated whether to suspend music totally from worship rather than reform it. In the end they decided to reform music (White, 2000).

It was Martin Luther, the German reformer, who saw the possibility of music in the liturgy. Luther was a musician and his German Mass of 1526 contains detailed instruction for singing the liturgy. He also urged that lay people should sing the ordinary parts of the Mass. He wrote hymns and produced a vernacular hymn book in 1524. Another famous Lutheran, the composer Johann Sebastian Bach (1685–1750) wrote great numbers of instrumental and choral pieces for the weekly Eucharist. He composed many chorales, for choirs and congregations, some based on non-biblical texts. He wrote what are known as choral cantatas (that is, meditations based on the lessons), oratorios (sacred dramas), and passions that tell the passion narrative (St Matthew and St John).

In Zurich the reformer Ulrich Zwingli felt compelled by unconditional obedience to Scripture to abandon music in worship, even though he was a musician himself. As a result of his influence singing ceased in Zurich churches in 1523.

> **TO DO**
>
> Listen to:
>
> * *Missa Papae Marcelli* by Palestrina (1555)
> * One of J. S. Bach's oratorios (Christmas, Easter or Ascension).
> * John Merbecke's setting for the Anglican liturgy
>
> What are the differences? Could any be used in a worship service? Which one lends itself best to an act of worship?

John Calvin dispensed with instrumental, choral and service music as well as hymns. He kept the singing of psalms, as they were 'inspired' texts, and he had them translated into French. All singing was congregational. Those who visited the services from other parts of the world were apparently impressed with the high degree of active participation and the solemnity and joy that psalmody gave to the services. The Presbyterian Church of Scotland adopted Calvin's view of only singing the psalms, arguing that only the words of Scripture are worthy to praise God. The English Puritans also held this view.

One consequence of the Protestant Reformation was the loss of the whole Latin musical repertory of both chant and polyphony, and the establishment of a new aesthetic of simple, memorable congregational song.

Isaac Watts, an English congregationalist in the late seventeenth and eighteenth century, wrote around 750 hymns. He is generally accepted as the Father of English hymnody, though he met stubborn resistance to his hymns and it was not until the nineteenth century that they were used by many Puritans.

Methodism emerged in the eighteenth century. Methodist congregations tended to be poor and consequently their churches had no organs. John Wesley opposed anthems because they were not 'joint worship', and there was no provision for service music. They did, however, have hymns. Since the framework for Methodist worship was within the national church and missional, John and Charles Wesley believed that hymns were an ideal way of reaching out to the unchurched. Hymns were not only to give praise to God but to teach doctrine.

Many parts of the Church of England in the mid-eighteenth-century used a variety of music, but very little hymnody. While there was no theological reason for this, psalm singing was the norm.

There was no place for the singing of metrical psalms in *The Book of Common Prayer*. At the time of its compilation music for services flourished especially in cathedrals and collegiate churches.

John Merbecke composed music for the Anglican Eucharist as early as 1550 and others, including William Byrd, Thomas Tallis and Orlando Gibbons, followed him.

Music and singing was not usually undertaken in parish churches, but concentrated in cathedrals and colleges. In *The Book of Common Prayer* 1662 there is an opportunity for an anthem based on Scripture or other texts to be sung after the third collect; as it states in the rubric, 'in quires and places where they sing' (Cummings, 2013).

In the nineteenth century, major musical changes took place in the Church of England. The pipe organ was introduced into many parish churches, and architectural changes increased the desire for parish choirs. Eventually the singing of hymns became popular and music was generally sung in harmony.

The Oxford Movement of the 1800s inspired renewed interest in liturgical music within the Church of England. John Jebb first drew attention to Merbecke's Prayer Book settings in 1841. In 1843, William Dyce published plainsong music for all the Anglican services, which included nearly all of Merbecke's settings adapted for the 1662 edition of *The Book of Common Prayer*. During the latter half of the nineteenth century, many different editions of Merbecke's settings were published, especially for the communion service, with arrangements by noted musicians such as John

Stainer, Charles Villiers Stanford and Basil Harwood. Merbecke's communion setting was very widely sung by choirs and congregations throughout the Anglican Communion until *The Book of Common Prayer* 1662 began to be supplanted by more modern liturgy in the late twentieth century (White, 2000).

The Roman Catholic Church during this period used a more operatic style of music, which needed highly trained choirs and professional musicians. Following Vatican II (1962–65), however, a revolution took place in church music. The Roman Catholic Church moved away from Gregorian chant to metrical hymnody. At first they borrowed from Protestant Churches, but in time hymns were written by Catholic musicians. The singing of psalms returned, with a cantor singing the verses and the congregation repeating a refrain.

Church music continues to grow. In services that are less formal and more in the style of praise and worship, music dominates for at least half the service with simple repetitive texts often projected on a screen. The texts are often based on single verses from Scripture and the musical instruments used include almost anything but a pipe organ. Seeker services usually have highly professional musicians and very little may be sung by the congregation.

In recent years the ecumenical community in Taizé, France, through the music of Jacques Berthier has developed a style of music that includes the repetition of simple texts, many scriptural, in different languages. The Iona Community in Scotland has developed a form of music through the Wild Goose worship group and the creativity of John Bell that highlights the issues of social justice. Both forms of music are rooted in theology and spirituality.

TO DO

Listen to music from the Taizé community and from the Iona Community. What makes them different and what makes them similar?

Choose one piece of music and reflect on its theology and on the spirituality that emerges from it.

Music and song in the liturgy

As Beth, Maggie and Paul continue their reflections on music and song, they raise the question about the value of music and singing in worship. They recognize that each of them has a different experience of music and singing in church services, but they agree that for all of them singing is important, and also listening to good music.

Gelineau (1992) suggests that 'singing and music take pride of place after words and gestures among all the signs and symbols that make up the liturgy'.

He goes on to say that singing or playing the organ are as much a part of the liturgy as reading a lesson or saying a prayer. He believes that the purpose of singing and music is to awaken meaning in the liturgy, suggesting that the liturgy is a 'festival gathering', and a festival implies singing, dancing and music.

White (2000) sees the chief function of music as adding a deeper dimension of participation in worship, saying that 'one of the reasons music aids worship is that music is a more expressive medium than ordinary speech' (p. 112).

As Paul, Maggie and Beth reflect on singing and music in the services, they appreciate the different forms of music in the churches they attend and realize that churches use music in different ways. For Paul hymns are very important, for Beth the settings of the Eucharist and the music at Evensong are important, and for Maggie it is worship songs that are important.

Paul sees hymns as a major part of worship, but he has not thought before about what hymns mean. White (1997) defines a hymn as any form of sacred poetry that is set to music for singing (usually by a congregation) in worship. For Paul the hymns of Isaac Watts, which include 'Jesus shall reign where'er the sun,' and 'O God, our help in ages past' and those by John and Charles Wesley are the bedrock of his faith. He realizes that it is through the singing of hymns that he reflects on his faith.

Paul talks about the preface to John Wesley's *Collection of Hymns for use of the people called Methodists*, where Wesley says that the hymnal should be 'a little body of experimental and practical divinity'. By this he meant that hymns should be a resource for theological reflection and spiritual development. For example, Charles Wesley's 'Hymn for Easter Day' (1739) reflects theologically on the resurrection.

Christ the Lord is ris'n today, Alleluia!
Sons of men and angels say, Alleluia!
Raise your joys and triumphs high, Alleluia!
Sing, ye heav'ns, and earth, reply, Alleluia!

Lives again our glorious King, Alleluia!
Where, O death, is now thy sting? Alleluia!
Once He died our souls to save, Alleluia!
Where thy victory, O grave? Alleluia!

Love's redeeming work is done, Alleluia!
Fought the fight, the battle won, Alleluia!
Death in vain forbids His rise, Alleluia!
Christ hath opened paradise, Alleluia!

Soar we now where Christ hath led, Alleluia!
Foll'wing our exalted Head, Alleluia!
Made like Him, like Him we rise, Alleluia!
Ours the cross, the grave, the skies, Alleluia!

Hail the Lord of earth and heaven, Alleluia!
Praise to Thee by both be given, Alleluia!
Thee we greet triumphant now, Alleluia!
Hail the Resurrection, thou, Alleluia!

King of glory, Soul of bliss, Alleluia!
Everlasting life is this, Alleluia!
Thee to know, Thy pow'r to prove, Alleluia!
Thus to sing, and thus to love, Alleluia!

Although Paul's experience of worship has included hymn singing, Beth's experience is different, and when she looks at the liturgies of her church, the Church of England, she notices how the current liturgies make space for music and recognizes that the older prayer books do not. In *The Book of Common Prayer* 1662 Beth sees that there is actually no provision for hymns.

The Book of Common Prayer 1662 proposes that the psalm may be said or sung, the *Te Deum* may be sung or said, the *Benedictus* or the *Jubilate Deo* may be sung, and the Apostles' Creed may be sung. There is also the provision for an anthem 'in quires and places where they sing'. The choice of canticles is limited, and that has been one of its criticisms. In *Common Worship* there is an extensive range of canticles for use at Morning and Evening Prayer on Sundays (Cummings, 2013).

As Beth thinks about the canticles she has heard both said and sung, she reflects on the fact that the word canticle means 'little song'. Canticles are based on the Scriptures and include biblical verses and biblical passages. They can also be hymns, that contain scriptural references, for example the Song of Moses (and Miriam) in Exodus 15 (below) and Luke's infancy narrative (Luke 1.46–55, 68–79; 2.29–32).

1   I will sing to the Lord, who has triumphed
      gloriously,
the horse and his rider he has thrown into the sea.
2   The Lord is my strength and my song
and has become my salvation.
3   This is my God whom I will praise,
the God of my forebears whom I will exalt.
4   The Lord is a warrior,
the Lord is his name.
5   Your right hand, O Lord, is glorious in power:
your right hand, O Lord, shatters the enemy.

6   At the blast of your nostrils, the sea covered
them;
they sank as lead in the mighty waters.
7   In your unfailing love, O Lord,
you lead the people whom you have redeemed.
8   And by your invincible strength
you will guide them to your holy dwelling.
9   You will bring them in and plant them, O Lord,
in the sanctuary which your hands have
established.

Exodus 15.1b–3, 6, 10, 13, 17 (Common Worship,
2011)

Some canticles have the appearance of songs, for
example Philippians 2.6–11 and Colossians 1.15–20.
Other passages tend to be acclamations, for example
Revelation 4.8, 4.11, 5.12–13, 7.12–13 and 15.3–4.
These have also formed the basis of canticles (Dawtry
and Headley, 2002).

Several of the *Common Worship* canticles come
from the monastic tradition and *Common Worship*
has drawn on the work of the Society of St Francis
and the canticles in *Celebrating Common Prayer*
(1992). The canticles used at Morning and Evening
Prayer are divided between opening canticles,
Old Testament canticles at Morning Prayer, New
Testament canticles at Evening Prayer and Gospel
canticles. The canticles in *Common Worship* vary

according to the season. The only canticles printed in full in the text are the *Benedictus* (below) and the *Magnificat,* taken from the opening chapters of Luke's Gospel.

1   Blessed be the Lord the God of Israel,
who has come to his people and set them free.
2   He has raised up for us a mighty Saviour,
born of the house of his servant David.
3   Through his holy prophets God promised of
    old
to save us from our enemies,
    from the hands of all that hate us,
4   To show mercy to our ancestors,
and to remember his holy covenant.
5   This was the oath God swore to our father
    Abraham:
to set us free from the hands of our enemies,
6   Free to worship him without fear,
holy and righteous in his sight
    all the days of our life.
7   And you, child, shall be called the prophet of
the Most High,
for you will go before the Lord to prepare his way,
8   To give his people knowledge of salvation
by the forgiveness of all their sins.
9   In the tender compassion of our God
the dawn from on high shall break upon us,

10 To shine on those who dwell in darkness and
the shadow of death,
and to guide our feet into the way of peace.
Luke 1.68–79 (Common Worship, 2011)

Beth has also enjoyed singing psalms and hearing
them being sung. The word 'psalm' comes from the
Greek word *psalmoi*, which means songs. The psalms
were the hymn book of Israel's Temple worship and
were used in various ways in the synagogue. For the
early Christians psalms were very much part of their
worship and would have been sung responsorially at
their community meals. The psalms have been used
since the fourth century as part of the liturgy of the
word at the Eucharist and as hymns of praise at the
daily offices.

A new psalter was prepared for *Common Worship*,
based on the psalter of the Episcopal Church of the
United States. The new psalter uses the 'you' form
of language and is generally inclusive of men and
women (Sinclair, 2002).

Maggie has been brought up on worship songs and
instrumental music. She is used to a less structured
service and an open style of worship that relies
heavily on the music of a band. The Old Testament
refers to the use of musical instruments. Moses, as
described in the book of Numbers, is encouraged
to make silver trumpets and to use them at their

appointed festivals. Flutes have had a place in the worship of the Temple, but not in the synagogue.

Instrumental music in Christian worship appears to have existed from the mid-second-century, but was short-lived as there came to be confusion between Christian and pagan music. The Canons attributed to St Basil (*c.* 330–379) for example, say: 'if one who reads the Scriptures in church learns to play the guitar, he shall confess it and if he does not return to playing it he shall suffer his penance for seven weeks. If he keeps playing it he shall be excommunicated and put out of the church' (White, 1997, p. 56).

In the 700s there emerged an instrument that dominated Christian worship for the next 13 centuries: the pipe organ. It was initially a simple instrument, but evolved to become more complex and ultimately to be known as the 'king of instruments' (White, 1997). In England in 1644 legislation was passed to dismantle all church organs, but with the restoration of the monarchy in 1660 the ban on liturgical use of instruments was rescinded and a great age of organ building began.

By the end of the eighteenth century, town bands began to be popular in churches. The various wind, brass and percussion instruments were played from the rear galleries of the churches to accompany congregational and choir singing. The use of musical instruments in worship continued to be a contentious issue, though, as they were associated with forms of secular music which expressed anti-religious themes.

Maggie reflects that today in the churches of which she has been part people use a variety of musical instruments to praise God. It is not unusual for Maggie to play the drums or the guitar in her music group. The music groups that have led worship in her experience have used the music of Graham Kendrick and others to encourage worship and to praise God.

TO DO

Visit two churches with varying forms of worship.

What is common in the liturgy?

Are psalms or canticles sung?

What hymns are sung?

Does the music and singing enhance the worship or detract from the worship?

Reflecting on your experience in the two churches, how does the experience differ from your home church?

Conclusion

This chapter has looked at the development of

music and song in the Church. It has explored how the writers of the New Testament used psalms and hymns to praise God. The chapter has reflected on the development of music and song in the light of different theological understandings.

Further reading

Dawtry, A. and Headley, C., 2002, 'A Service of the Word' in P. Bradshaw (ed.), *Companion to Common Worship*, Vol. 1 pp. 52–84, London:SPCK.

Gelineau, J., 1992, 'Music and Singing in the Liturgy', in C. Jones, G. Wainwright, E. Yarnold and P. Bradshaw (eds), *The Study of Liturgy*, revised edition, pp. 493–507, London: SPCK.

Sinclair, J., 2002, 'The Psalter', in P. Bradshaw (ed.) *Companion to Common Worship*, Vol. 1, pp.236–8, London:SPCK

Wesley J., 1889, *Collection of Hymns for the use of the people called Methodists*. London: Wesleyan-Methodist Book-room.

White, J. F., 2000, *Introducing Christian Worship*, Nashville, TN: Abingdon Press.

White, S. J., 1997, *Groundwork of Christian Worship*, Peterborough: Epworth Press.

www.churchofengland.org/prayer-and-worship/ worship-texts-and-resources/common-worship/ common-material/canticles/song-moses-and-miriam-easter

8

Movement and Space

Paul, Beth and Maggie are having a conversation about movement and space in the liturgy. They bring different perspectives from their church backgrounds: Paul from a Methodist church, Beth from an Anglo-Catholic church and Maggie from an evangelical Anglican church. As they begin to talk they realize that movement within the liturgical year is important to the life of the Church. They reflect on the Easter season, and the journey from Advent, to Christmas, to Epiphany, and then through Candlemas to Lent and on to Easter.

They also talk about the rhythms and movement in life, from birth, to childhood, the teenage years, to young adults, to middle age, to old age and finally to death. As they think about the liturgical year and the life cycle, they recognize the connection between stages of life and the liturgical year. They reflect on the birth of Jesus, his baptism, his ministry, his death and his resurrection. They recognize that Christian worship uses time as one of its essential structures. The present time is used to reflect God's acts in the past and in the future. The liturgical year is a movement from Christ's incarnation, his birth, through to his ascension into heaven, and the coming of the Holy Spirit.

Paul, Beth and Maggie also reflect on the fact that the Church has liturgies that move people through different rites of passage. Within their local churches there are liturgies to mark certain stages in life: giving thanks for the birth of a child, celebrating baptism, confirmation and marriage; and prayers for the end of life, culminating in the funeral rite.

TO DO

Think about your church building; how is the space divided up?

Does that space tell you something about the past and about the present of your church's liturgy?

Think of the church year; which season is most important to you?

How does your church reflect the movement of the liturgical year?

As Paul, Beth and Maggie continue to talk to each other they realize that all these acts of worship and rites of passage are undertaken in a particular space, whether that be a church building, or other building, or a pilgrimage site. They realize that architecturally religious buildings can be very different from each other and this difference is accounted for by the emphasis the church places on particular parts of the liturgy. If their church is more word-based, then the building will focus on the pulpit; if their church is more sacramentally based the emphasis will be on the altar.

The movement of the liturgical year

Beth talks with Paul and Maggie about the Christian calendar. She begins by reflecting on the fact that there are two overall cycles in the Christian calendar. The first is the calendar of times and seasons of the year, and is known as the *Temporale*. This Latin word refers to the seasons of the year, which include Advent and Easter, and what several traditions now call 'Ordinary Time'. The second calendar celebrates the saints' days through the year, and this is referred to as the *Sanctorale*. In the early centuries, the death of a Christian martyr would be commemorated annually on the date of the death with a service at the graveside, including a celebration of the Lord's Supper. Lists of local martyrs were circulated among the various Christian communities and eventually the date of the martyr's death was marked throughout the Church as a whole (White, 1997). Within the Anglican Church the saints' days have been divided into 'Red Letter' days – the principal celebrations – and 'Black Letter' days – lesser observances (Gordon-Taylor, 2002).

The *Temporale* calendar has two key focal points, or *kairos* times. *Kairos* times means time with a content, and the content is invariably related to salvation. The two key focal points are the birth and the death/resurrection of Jesus (White, 1997). Easter was originally the only annual festival of the Christian Church, and celebrated both the death and resurrection of Christ in a single feast. It was celebrated annually to coincide with the Jewish Passover. Some scholars believe it to have begun in apostolic times, while others see it emerging in the second century. By the end of the second century most Christian churches had agreed to keep Easter on the Sunday nearest to the Passover.

From the end of the second century churches in North Africa and Rome used Easter as a time for baptisms. The Easter liturgy was preceded by fasting, for one, two or even more days. There was a vigil of readings and prayer through Saturday night, with baptisms and the Eucharist at cockcrow on Easter Sunday (Gordon-Taylor, 2002).

By the end of the third century there were three commemorations: Epiphany, Pascha and Pentecost. Included in the Epiphany celebrations was the birth of Christ, the annunciation, the visit of the Magi, the presentation of Jesus in the Temple, the various miracles that witnessed to Jesus' identity, his baptism by John, and the calling of the disciples

(White, 1997). By the end of the fourth century Epiphany had become four commemorations: Christmas, the circumcision of Christ, the Epiphany, and the presentation of Christ. Pascha becomes five commemorations: Palm Sunday, Maundy Thursday, Good Friday, Holy Saturday and Easter Day; and Pentecost consisted of two: Ascension and Pentecost.

Lent was first referred to as 'forty days' at the Council of Nicaea in AD 325; it immediately precedes Easter and begins with Ash Wednesday. The Easter season extends for 50 days through to the Day of Pentecost. At first these 50 days were far more important than the 40 days of Lent. The resurrection is commemorated by a day each week, Sunday, by a festival each year, Easter Day, and by an Easter season.

The most significant development in the fourth-century calendar was Holy Week. Ceremonies were developed reflecting the last days of Jesus' life, including Palm Sunday, the commemoration of the last supper with foot-washing on Maundy Thursday, and the veneration of the cross on Good Friday with three hours of vigil. Easter Eve is the climax of the whole year as the Church gathers in darkness for the Easter Vigil before celebrating the resurrection at first light.

There were few changes of note to the calendar after the fourth century. Trinity Sunday was introduced about AD 1000; unlike other feasts, it represents a theological doctrine unrelated to a historical event.

Beth is keen to share her experience of the liturgical year, with its movement from the birth of Jesus to his death, resurrection and ascension, with Paul and Maggie. Maggie has very little experience of the Holy Week and Easter ceremonies but reflects that the movement of Holy Week is so important to the understanding of the last few days of Christ's life. Paul can see how important movement is in the Christian year, but his experience is that of John Wesley's calendar, which did not include Lent or Holy Week. It did include Advent, Christmas, Good Friday, Easter, Ascension Day, Trinity Sunday and All Saints' Day.

TO DO

Attend one of the major festivals of the Church's year and reflect on its place in the liturgical calendar and how it moves people through the life of Christ and their own journey of faith.

Beth, Maggie and Paul can see that theologically the Christian calendar helps the Church and its members proclaim Jesus Christ until he comes again, and testifies to the indwelling of the Holy Spirit in the Church (White, 2000). Over the history of the Christian Church, the calendar has been adjusted at various times to suit the theology of different churches. At the Reformation, some churches abolished the calendar but the Church of England kept a simplified version of it. *The Book of Common Prayer* 1549 and subsequent prayer books had a reduced number of ceremonies and variable seasonal texts such as collects, readings and eucharistic prefaces (Cummings, 2013).

The 1928 proposed revision of *The Book of Common Prayer* retained the basic pattern of seasons and major festivals with some minor adjustments and improvements. One controversial addition was the commemoration of All Souls on 2 November.

The work of the Liturgical Commission in the 1950s eventually led to the calendar of *The Alternative Service Book 1980,* which included post-Reformation saints and a new two-year lectionary. This began the Christian year on the ninth Sunday before Christmas and changed the practice of counting the Sundays after Trinity to counting the Sundays after Pentecost.

The publication of *Lent, Holy Week, Easter: Services and prayers* (Church of England, 1986) and *The Promise of His Glory: For the seasons from All Saints to Candlemas* (Church of England, 1991) showed a movement towards broadening the liturgical year and providing the resources for services appropriate to the season.

Since the publication of *The Alternative Service*

Book 1980 the number of principal holy days (which included Ash Wednesday, Maundy Thursday and Good Friday) has increased to include the Presentation of Christ, the Annunciation, Trinity Sunday and All Saints' Day. There are around 26 festivals in the Church's calendar and a very large number of lesser festivals.

The principal holy days, the festivals and lesser festivals that make up the liturgical year help to order time within the liturgical life of the Church. The Christian week also witnesses to time and movement. For the people of Israel, the sabbath was the seventh day of the week and was set aside as a day of rest. The sabbath was not only a commemoration of God's rest at the conclusion of creation but a continual reminder to the Jews of their own liberation from oppression by a just and righteous God (White, 1997). For Christianity the sabbath became the first day of the week, the day of resurrection. In Christian theology, just as God had begun the creation of the world on the first day of the week, so too had God begun the new creation with the resurrection, on the first day of the week (White, 1997).

Operating within the calendar is the lectionary. The lectionary is a set of Scripture lessons based on the Christian year. The most frequently used lectionary these days is the Revised Common Lectionary, which is designed to cover a three-year period, and the years are designated A, B and C.

The church year begins on Advent Sunday. For each Sunday or festival, three lessons are appointed: the first is usually from the Old Testament, the second usually from an epistle, and the third is always from a Gospel. After Easter, lessons from Acts are read in place of the epistle as the story of the new creation begins with resurrection. Over the course of three years, when all three lessons are used, passages will have been selected from most of the books in the New Testament and from many of the books in the Old Testament. The lectionary guides the choices appropriate for any given Sunday and allows the service to develop a connected theme for its prayers, sermon and music.

Beth is all too aware of the lectionary as she is a reader in her church. Paul recognizes that some of his ministers use the lectionary on occasions, but like Maggie he also sees the minister choosing readings to fit in with the preaching series.

The calendar and the lectionary within it allow people to experience and journey through the Christian year from Advent in one year to Advent in the next. It allows the life of Jesus to be told from birth to death, through resurrection to ascension. The calendar and the lectionary within in it order time and give movement.

TO DO

Visit two or three churches of different denominations. What do you notice that is different in the sacred space? How does this inform you of what is important to the worshipping life of the community?

Paul, Beth and Maggie now talk about the different ways in which their churches have been constructed. Beth's church is very traditional, built in the shape of the cross with an area known as the sanctuary where the choir and eucharistic ministers sit. The altar is the focus in the church and the pews are in rows facing the altar. There is a high altar behind a screen, but the church has been reordered to include a nave altar that stands closer to the congregation. Paul's church has a small altar table, but a large pulpit. People's eyes are drawn to the pulpit rather than to the altar. Maggie's church has a stage at the front for the worship group. There is also a lectern from which the worship leader or preacher takes the service or preaches. The congregation sits on chairs facing the staging area. Paul, Beth and Maggie reflect on their space and recognize that for all of them the space in which they worship is sacred.

Sacred space has been an important part of both the Jewish and the Christian religions. Sacred space is understood as a place where believers can encounter God in a special way. From Abraham in the Old Testament to the present day there are stories about people whose encounter with God stirs in them the desire to name and set apart places as holy and to identify them by the building of an altar of sacrifice (Giles, 1999). Moses is commanded in Exodus (20.24–25) to make the altar and informed that there will be no limitation of time and space in honouring God. Exodus gives precise instructions (chapters 24 to 31) for the construction of the altar. More important than the altar, however, is the ark and instructions are given on how this was to be made, in order to house the tablets of stone on which the law has been written. The ark becomes a meeting place between God and the people of God, but this is not to be in one specific place since the instructions given by God are to build an ark that is portable. This portability is seen through the provision of a tent of meeting that was to be erected over the ark. The concept of a holy place is given a new dynamic in the understanding of a God who journeys with the people of God (Giles, 1999). From the time of Abraham the Jewish people were called to a nomadic lifestyle, and this was later part of Jesus' spiritual tradition; he also embraced a peripatetic ministry.

While the Jewish people were called to a nomadic life, the eleventh century BC saw the emergence of the monarchy and a move to enshrine the ark in a permanent structure. The Temple was built by Solomon in about 922 BC and it soon became the only place where sacrifices would take place. People now began to make pilgrimages to the Temple and the structure of the building with its many courts surrounding the holy of holies reinforced the rigidly hierarchical system by which the Jewish people approached God.

In 587 BC the Temple was destroyed by the Babylonians and the Israelites were taken into exile, so changing the focus of their sacred space. In the years of exile the Jews built synagogues to maintain their religious identity. The synagogue, which literally means 'gathering', became the place of religious meetings on sabbaths and holy days where the Jewish people gathered to study the law and pray. The home for the Jewish people was also a sacred place where prayer and blessings were offered. On their return from exile 70 years later they rebuilt the Temple even more magnificently, only for it to be destroyed by the Romans in AD 70. The synagogue by the time of Jesus was a place for regular meetings on the sabbath and other holy days. A synagogue was found in practically every settlement and was the scene for many of Jesus' important messages.

TO DO

Reflecting on your own life, where do you feel the presence of God? Is it in a particular place or is it in a set of criteria that may be met in a number of places?

After the death of Jesus the first Christians continued to use the synagogues, the Temple and people's homes. Eventually they moved away from the synagogue and Temple and worshipped in the homes of wealthy Christians and to a lesser extent in the catacombs. This era was known as the domestic Church. Larger houses of this period had the space needed for worshipping communities; they were generally in the style of a series of rooms grouped around an open courtyard.

The Christian community in this period travelled light and as late as the third century there were still no static buildings. It was in the fourth century with the conversion of the Emperor Constantine to Christianity that the need for bigger meeting places arose. The Church chose to meet in the basilica, or hall of the king. The basilica was an imposing civic building, traditionally rectangular with an apse at both ends. The length of the basilica lent itself to processions which aligned itself with the imperial nature of the building and the state (Giles, 1999). The basilica plan was altered by the Christians; the apse was to be found at the east end only. It contained the bishop's chair and benches at either side for his presbyters. The altar was a wooden, free-standing structure placed in front of the apse. The ambo or reading desk stood in the middle of the people, while the font was in a separate place, the baptistry.

As Christians grew in numbers and status so did their buildings. The basilica plan continued to be used in the West, while the Church in the East, centred around Constantinople, developed buildings that were square rather than rectangular. The magnificent domes that covered them gave to these interiors an openness and space. Liturgy within these buildings was also different. In the East there was a more communal understanding of the Christian community at worship than in the West, where a more hierarchical system developed (Giles, 1999).

The internal layout of the church buildings in the West continued to change with the move away from a community at worship towards a professional clergy. The altar was placed away from the people, in the apse. The apse was renamed the sanctuary, and a canopy or ciborium was placed within the sanctuary and surrounded by low walls. The nave area, where liturgical activity like reading Scripture took place, was also demarcated by low walls. As the role of the lone priest developed and that of other ministers declined so all liturgical furniture moved into the sanctuary.

The church building became a visual aid for the Christian message. Transepts were added to basilicas and this produced a ground plan of the building in the form of a cross. The subdivided interiors of churches in the West reinforced a developing ecclesiology in which order and hierarchy was important.

The Middle Ages saw the establishment of highly specialized types of churches: pilgrim churches or shrines, churches for monastic communities, collegiate churches, cathedrals, preaching churches, and ordinary parish churches. The monastic communities in particular developed the space in churches to suit the needs of their community. Since they spent a large part of their time singing and saying the daily offices, a functional type of building evolved specially designed to suit this style of worship. The most important space was the choir stalls, arranged in two parallel facing sections so that psalms could be sung antiphonally (alternate voices back and forth). The altar was positioned at the east end for Mass and a screen sectioned off the nave.

Parish churches followed a similar design, with large screened chancels where the clergy led worship while the lay people remained in the nave. In the nave was also positioned a pulpit around which the people could stand. Unlike the monastic church, though, each parish church contained a font.

Until the fourteenth century the nave was an empty space where people could move around in order to see and hear the liturgy. The introduction of pews led to an individualized approach to prayer and religion. Beth can identify with this form of church. Her own church, built in the Victorian period, is laid out in the same fashion with a clear demarcation, a rood screen, between the priest and the people.

The Protestant Reformation and the Roman Catholic Counter-Reformation saw great changes in churches. The Jesuit order, founded in 1540 as the Society of Jesus, which had no need for choir space to say the daily office together, led the way among Roman Catholics in building sumptuous churches where the Mass could be seen in all its glory. Without the choir or screen the altar table was clearly visible (White, 2000). The Protestants began constructing numerous new buildings, many designed in the centralized shape without a chancel. A characteristic Protestant addition was the balcony, to enable speakers to be heard by a larger number of people. The balconies helped bring the total community together around the pulpit and Lord's table, although movement was difficult. The Methodist church that Paul attends has balconies and he recognizes the structure that focuses on the pulpit and the preaching of the word.

The nineteenth century saw the revival of styles of architecture from the past, particularly imitations of classical Greek and medieval Gothic buildings, and these styles gave shape to the experience of Christian worship. White (1997) writes:

> Each of these styles began as attempts to provide suitable expressions of a particular understanding of Christian worship: the lightness and simplicity of classical design for those who saw worship as a rational and well-ordered form of public service, and the lofty mystery of the Gothic for those who viewed worship as a transcendent experience of divine–human encounter. (p. 77)

The church building inhabited today tells a story of its past and its present. The rituals associated with worship, as White suggests, influence the way church buildings were designed and built. Over the past 50 years the liturgical movement has tried to address God in language and forms appropriate to the time in which the Church now finds itself. The liturgical movement has tried to embrace both worship and the environment of worship; ritual patterns and the buildings that house them. Giles (1996), in his book *Re-pitching the Tent: Reordering the church building for worship and mission*, draws on his experience of reordering a church in Huddersfield and the experience of congregations in widely differing local cultures in North America and Europe. Giles argues that 'each liturgical space is a particular response of a local community of faith unique in God's sight' (p. 143). He goes on to say:

> This in turn means that in liturgical design we are not primarily concerned with designing a series of 'objects' (font, ambo, altar etc), but with creating a space in which the 'subject' (the assembly itself) can give full and deep expression to its life in the Risen Christ. (p. 143)

Giles suggests that the Christian community should learn from the theatre and the stage designer. The stage designer sets the scene, and creates the space. He develops his argument by looking at the different spaces in the church building in the context of liturgy. He explores the gathering space as a 'hearth' around which the community of faith gathers, relaxes and feels at home. Giles looks at the initiation space and how important it is to welcome people into the Christian community by having a space that helps people understand the Christian life as a journey. The font should therefore not be in a corner but 'in a place of permanent significance clearly demarcated from the rest of the area of liturgical assembly' (p. 167).

As people in the Christian community continue their journey, having gathered and having reflected on their baptismal vocations, they now move on to 'the place of the word' before approaching the altar for the breaking of bread. Each of these physical spaces reflects the movement of thought and practice. The place of the word is more than the ambo; it is a place where people 'are chastened and comforted, challenged and exhilarated by the word of God' (p. 174).

REFLECTING ON EXPERIENCE

In what ways does the community to which you belong pay honour to the word of God? In what ways may greater prominence be given to the word?

Giles continues his understanding of journey emphasizing the need for movement in liturgy and finding the 'best' liturgical space for different parts of the eucharistic service. He advocates being sensitive to both the liturgy and the space in which the liturgy takes place.

Conclusion

This chapter has explored the idea of movement and space. Movement in terms of the development of a Christian calendar moves people through the Scriptures and through the life cycle of the Christian year. This is a movement that takes people from life to death. It has also looked at the 'sacred space' in which people worship and how the building has changed and developed over the centuries.

Further reading

Bradshaw, P. (ed.), 2002, *Companion to Common Worship*, Vol 1, London: SPCK.

Giles, R., 1996, *Re-pitching the Tent*, Norwich: Canterbury Press.

White, J. F., 2000, *Introducing Christian Worship*, Nashville, TN: Abingdon Press.

White, S. J., 1997, *Groundwork of Christian Worship*, Peterborough: Epworth Press.

9

Seeing, Smelling, Touching

Paul, Beth and Maggie are having a conversation about using the senses in worship. They bring different perspectives from their different church backgrounds: Paul coming from a Methodist church, Beth from an Anglo-Catholic church, and Maggie from an evangelical Anglican church. They reflect on the fact that a lot of the Church's liturgy is word-based and cerebral. They recognize that the symbolic and non-verbal in liturgy has been lost in many churches and that more often than not people do things and enact rituals without understanding why.

Paul recounts the fact that in his church some people in the choir turn and face east when they recite the creed. He has no idea why they do that. Beth talks about her church and the Gospel procession. The Gospel is read halfway down the aisle, among the people, and she is aware that while some people turn and face the Gospel, others keep staring in front of them with the reading taking place behind them. Maggie talks about the visual things that she has seen when visiting cathedrals: the colours of the altar frontal, the statues and the icons. She has often wondered how these can help in worship.

For Paul Christianity is a religion of the word. The written word has been important to him in his journey of faith, but of course he is also aware that, as John's Gospel says, the Word was made flesh and dwelt among us. He knows that Jesus turned water into wine, made the blind see and the mute speak, washed the feet of fishermen, and broke bread with unsavoury characters.

Paul reflects on the psalmists and their understanding that words were not the only way to worship God. The psalmists' songs suggest that dancing, animals, birds, trees, oil and wine all speak in their various ways of God's infinite wisdom, beauty and love. The trees praise God with their seasonal dressing and undressing, the mountain goats praise God as they bring forth their light-footed young, and the bread and wine and oil speak of God's sustaining love that is worth savouring.

Paul, Beth and Maggie begin to realize that the senses are very important in worshipping God. After all, Beth says, in the words of Thomas Aquinas (a medieval philosopher and theologian of the thirteenth century) in his *Summa Theologica*, everything in the mind has its origins in the senses.

As Paul, Beth and Maggie think about the history of the Church they discover that it was the Reformation in the sixteenth century that put an end to elaborate and lengthy eucharistic services. Paul comments that the liturgy of the post-Reformation churches became simple, less ornate and more word-based. In recent years, liturgists have tried to develop worship that takes into account all the senses.

TO DO

Reflect upon your own experience of using your senses in worship.

Are the services you attend more word-based?

In what ways are your senses stimulated in worship?

Does the stimulation enhance your worshipping experience?

Perham (1992), in his book *Liturgy Pastoral and Parochial*, talks about liturgy being more than words. In worship every sense is used: 'we see, we hear, we touch, we smell' (p. 24). Light, colour, music, movement and incense are used to help aid worship. Perham goes on to say: 'It is the whole self that is offered to God, and those who plan worship should see that all senses are effectively employed' (pp. 24–5). Bianchi (2002) also says that liturgy, especially the liturgy of the Eucharist, is

> an experience that involves all of the believer's senses. Those who participate listen to the word of God proclaimed, see icons, candles, and the

faces of those around them, taste the eucharist bread and wine, smell incense, and touch their neighbours, as they exchange the sign of peace... the celebration of this mystery involves all the senses, but requires that they be refined and transfigured so that we can perceive all reality 'in Christ'. The senses are not eliminated, but ordered by faith, trained in prayer, grafted in Christ, and transfigured by the Holy Spirit. (pp. 9–10)

Gray-Reeves and Perham (2011) in their book *The Hospitality of God* talk of five characteristics of emergent church worship. One of these characteristics says that liturgy needs to be multi-sensory and have complexity:

Emerging churches take seriously the need to employ the senses, and especially the recovery of the visual. Worship should present a variety of options for people to express themselves and offer something forward by way of art, reflection, prayer, study or meditation. (p. 23)

Worship in the Old Testament engaged all the five senses. The Jewish prayer *Shema Yisrael* begins, 'Hear, O Israel...' (Deuteronomy 6.4). In the New Testament the physical senses were important in the formation of the relationships between Jesus and those who came to believe in him. Luke 19.1–10 reveals how Zacchaeus needed to have sight of Jesus in order to believe. The story of Thomas (John 20.24–25) reveals how he needed to touch Jesus before he could believe.

Throughout the centuries many have encountered Christ through their senses. Perham (1992), Bianchi (2002), and Gray-Reeves and Perham (2011) argue that worship when done well is a full-body experience. Songs, hymns and psalms are sung, Scripture is read and listened to, sermons are heard, and the Eucharist is celebrated. People sit, stand and taste the bread and wine of Holy Communion. The church is adorned in different colours and the minister or priest wears coloured vestments according to the season. All this adds to the sensory worship experience. As Paul, Beth and Maggie explore the senses in worship they begin by discussing the sense of sight.

Seeing: the sense of sight

Within the Scriptures there are many references to God being revealed and communicating with human beings through the sense of sight. God's promise to Noah in the Old Testament is communicated through the sign of a rainbow (Genesis 9.11–14). God communicated the message of deliverance of Moses through a burning bush (Exodus 3.1–7) and then brought the people out of Egypt by parting the Red Sea (Exodus 14.19–21).

At the baptism of Jesus a descending dove appears to communicate the Spirit at Jesus' baptism (Matthew 3.13–17). Paul's conversion experience happened through a blinding light (Acts 9.3). Sight was an important sense in both the Old and New Testaments, not least in the many references to seeing the works of God. Sight was a sense valued by Jesus himself and this is evidenced by the number of times he gives sight back to the people, whether that be literally or metaphorically.

In the Early Church, the sense of sight was a valuable means of perception and communication. The decoration of house churches and the catacombs depict stories from the Bible, so communicating the miracles of Jesus and salvation as retold through both the Old Testament and the New Testament. As religion moved into the public sphere with the acceptance of Christianity by the Emperor Constantine, so the visual in the basilicas became important. The evidence for the importance of the visual was the increased number of inscriptions and paintings on the walls and the raised altar at the apse end of the church which would help facilitate the congregation's view. In the medieval period, however, the importance of allowing people to see declined and screens were built, obscuring the congregation's view of the liturgical action.

After the Reformation the emphasis in the Protestant tradition was on hearing rather than seeing. Later there was a move back towards using the sense of sight in worship, for instance with the Catholic Liturgical Movement in the mid-nineteenth century and the return of colour to the inside of churches.

Beth has grown up in a church where ritual and symbolism are very much part of the life of the church. She recognizes the different colours of the vestments and liturgical hangings. She knows how the church calendar is worked out through the different colours of the altar frontals, the pulpit fall and the vestments the ministers wear.

Liturgical colours first became significant in medieval times. The first real evidence of a connection between liturgical seasons and particular colours is the Augustinian Canons of the Latin Church in Jerusalem in the eleventh century (Gordon-Taylor, 2002). It was not, however, until 1570, that a defined formal set of colours for liturgical use was drawn up by Pope Pius V. His sequence of colours forms the basis of those still used in both the Roman Catholic and the Anglican Church.

At the Reformation the reformers associated liturgical colours with Rome and consequently saw little significance in them for their churches. The Lutheran Church and the Church of England preserved them in a limited way. The Oxford Movement in the nineteenth century gave the liturgical colours a firm place in the Anglican Church (Gordon-Taylor, 2002).

In the twentieth century colours began to be associated with the mood of particular seasons: drab colours like purple for times of penitence, white and gold for festivals, red for martyrs, green and yellow for growth and renewal. Black is used in the Anglican Church for funerals and requiem Eucharists. *The Alternative Service Book 1980* was the first publication to set out an authorized scheme of colour, which has continued into *Common Worship*.

Colourful vestments, altar frontals and pulpit falls are important not just to observe the changing season within the liturgy but also as an outward expression to the specific character of the mysteries being celebrated. White is used for the birth of Jesus and his resurrection, thus associating white with a time of celebration; purple is used for Advent and Lent, thus associating purple with times of penitence. As Gordon-Taylor (2002) says:

> In this way it (colour) has a place in worship, where creation's loving response to the creator is most typically expressed. This suggests that where liturgical colours are used, careful consideration ought to be given to context and quality, lest what has the potential to be a powerful sign of the interplay of human and divine love become an empty piece of ritual. (p. 46)

TO DO

What is your experience of liturgical colour in your church?

Do the liturgical hangings change with the seasons?

Do you find that seeing different colours helps you to reflect on the festival or seasons within the life of the Church?

What are the positives and negatives to colour being used in this way?

Giles (2004) in *Creating Uncommon Worship* talks about the importance of the senses in worship. In relation to sight he says that if we don't want 'cerebral purity and sensory renunciation' (p. 79) then visual beauty as a stimulus to our senses and emotions is important in the context of the church and in the liturgy.

Paul, Beth and Maggie continue to reflect on their experience of using their sight in worship and as they do this they turn their attention to the sense of touch and worship.

Touching: the sense of touch

Paul, Beth and Maggie think of the importance of touch and how it informs the person about the nature of the world. Maggie says that touch helps protect people through the sensory data in their bodies. She gives the example of touching something hot and our automatic instinct to move or even jump away. Beth says that touch also helps us receive the emotional information that we need to thrive, to develop full mental, emotional and social intelligence. The three of them recognize that touch is important to the well-being of people, and as they reflect on the Old Testament they realize that the Hebrew people understood people to be whole and that included their senses.

In the Old Testament the prophet Amos says: 'the Lord of hosts, he who touches the earth and it melts, and all who live in it mourn...' (Amos 9.5). It is the touch of God that confirms Isaiah's forgiveness and establishes him as a prophet: 'The seraph touched my mouth with it and said...' (Isaiah 6.7). For Isaiah the sense of God's touch is both a way of experience and information.

In the New Testament, throughout Jesus' public ministry he touched people and they touched him. In Matthew's Gospel people 'begged him that they might touch even the fringe of his cloak; and all who touched it were healed' (Matthew 14.36). In Jesus' ministry touch becomes an important sign of the real physical connection between human beings and God (Richards, 2007).

Jesus heals through touch, by laying his hands on people in pain or suffering. The laying on of hands continues in the liturgy of healing and reconciliation:

> In the name of God and trusting in his might alone,
> Receive Christ's healing touch to make you whole.
> May Christ bring you wholeness
> Of body, mind and spirit,
> Deliver you from every evil,
> And give you his peace.
> Amen.
> (*Common Worship: Pastoral Services*, 2000, pp. 21, 33, 93)

Paul remembers an occasion when he went to a service of healing in his own church, where there was the laying on of hands. In *The Methodist Worship Book* (1999) there is a choice of three texts that accompany the laying on of hands and or anointing with oil.

> *Either*
> Father,
> Send your spirit of life and health on your servant,
> N; the name of Christ Amen.
> *Or*
> N, the grace of Christ brings you wholeness and gives you peace. Amen.

Or
May the Spirit of the living God
Present with us now,
Heal you of all that harms you,
In body mind or spirit;
In the name of Jesus Christ Amen.
(*The Methodist Worship Book*, 1999, p. 413)

The New Testament offers a number of accounts that emphasize that healing is ministered in the name of Jesus.

Touch is important to belief particularly after the resurrection of Jesus. Jesus said to the disciples, 'Look at my hands and my feet; see that it is I myself. Touch me and see' (Luke 24.39). Touch in the Gospel tradition is used to convey health and comfort and as a means of communication. For example, after the resurrection Thomas makes it clear that 'Unless I see the mark of the nails in his hands, and put my finger in the mark of the nails and my hand in his side, I will not believe' (John 20.25). The risen Christ needed to be communicated through touch.

As the Church developed through the centuries, however, the sense of 'touch' lost its spontaneity and warmth. It ceased to be a way for perceiving and conveying health and comfort and became ritualized, formalized, and clericalized. After the apostolic age there was very little in the liturgy that specifically emphasized touch. Even the 'kiss of peace' became no more than a form of words.

The ritual of sharing the peace goes back to New Testament times with the call in Romans 16.16 to 'Greet one another with a holy kiss.' Giles (2004) in *Creating Uncommon Worship* says that 'The peace is no mere gesture, however, for it embodies that reconciliation one with another that Jesus taught was a prerequisite of our eligibility to offer worship' (Giles, 2004, pp. 135-7).

In the Anglican Church *The Book of Common Prayer* 1552 removed the peace from the liturgy and it did not return until 1928 as an option after the eucharistic prayer. In *Series Two* it was still optional, placed before the eucharistic prayer, while in *Series Three* it became mandatory. Both *The Alternative Service Book 1980* and *Common Worship* retain the peace with the option of a number of sentences to introduce it (Bradshaw, Giles and Kershaw, 2002).

As Paul, Beth and Maggie talk about the peace they recognize that for some older members of their congregations the peace is difficult. They don't like shaking hands with others, let alone giving the kiss of peace; while for others, especially in Maggie's church, the peace can become rather exuberant. Beth suggests that for people on their own the peace may be the only occasion in the week when they touch another human being and have human contact.

As Paul, Beth and Maggie continue with this reflection they think about the other liturgies of the church when people are touched: in baptism, in marriage, at funerals. During ordination services bishops, priests and deacons are touched with the laying on of hands, or the imposition of oil, a sign of apostolic succession; and in communion lips and hands are touched.

In baptism water is felt on the skin, an experience of touch that speaks directly of washing and becoming clean. Beth mentions the tradition in her church of using holy water to cross yourself as you enter the building as a reminder of baptism and the promises made at baptism. At confirmation, ordination, commissioning or consecration hands may be laid on Christian people.

In the Ash Wednesday liturgy, Christians may be touched with ash, which reminds them that we are created from dust and to dust we shall return:

Dear friends in Christ,
I invite you to receive these ashes
as a sign of the spirit of penitence with which we
   shall keep this season of Lent.
God our Father,
you create us from the dust of the earth:
grant that these ashes may be for us
a sign of our penitence

and a symbol of our mortality;
for it is by your grace alone
that we receive eternal life
in Jesus Christ our Saviour. **Amen.**

*The president and people receive the imposition of
ashes*
At the imposition the minister says to each person

Remember that you are dust, and to dust you
    shall return.
Turn away from sin and be faithful to Christ.
(*Common Worship: Times and Seasons*, 2006)

Chrism oil, blessed by the bishop during the Chrism
Mass, is used in various acts of anointing and healing
within the sacraments, and the laying on of hands
is an important part of Christian healing services.
Rites of preparation for death involve touching the
physical body in blessing and anointing. Touch also
mediates the sense of veneration. On Good Friday
people may kiss or touch the feet of Jesus on the
cross. On Maundy Thursday feet are touched as
they are washed in memory of Christ washing the
disciples' feet in the account in John's Gospel.

Beth thinks about her priest who kisses the altar,
the stole, the gospel. She explains about the Eucharist
in her church where the priest uses touch to remind

people of the experienced reality of the Last Supper. Hands are washed and dried, the elements of bread and wine are touched and handled. Hands perform the acts of consecration. In the Eucharist people are touched in the receiving of the bread and wine, the body and blood of Christ (Richards, 2007).

TO DO

Look at John 20 and the story of Thomas. Do you think Thomas actually touched Jesus? Search on Google for artworks depicting this story. Do the artists actually show Thomas touching Jesus?

Paul, Maggie and Beth continue in their discussions, thinking about the sense of smell.

Smelling: the sense of smell

The sense of smell, Hawes writes in *Sense and Nonsense in Worship*, has been used 'more metaphorically than literally in Christian literature and liturgy'. There are many references in the Old Testament to smell and fragrance. In Exodus 16.24 the Hebrews used their sense of smell to test the freshness of the manna, and in Leviticus (26.31) and Amos (5.21) God uses this sense to show displeasure and rejection of the offerings made to him.

The sense of smell in the Old Testament is mostly apparent in the use of incense. In the Old Testament incense was used in the Israelite Temple as an act of worship and a way of communicating with God. The offering of incense symbolized the ascension of prayers to God. The use of incense would have engaged the sense of smell. In Exodus the priest is instructed to burn 'fragrant incense' each morning and evening on the altar of incense (Exodus 30.7). The prophet Malachi calls people to bring 'pure offerings and incense' (Malachi 1.11). In the New Testament Zechariah learnt about the birth of his son, John the Baptist, during a time when he was offering incense to the Lord (Luke 1.8–22). Incense was a medium of communication in biblical worship that called people's attention to God; it was an aid in worship.

Beth talks to Paul and Maggie about the use of incense in her church, about the censing of the altar and the people during the liturgy of Holy Communion. She also reflects on the use of incense during Evening Prayer.

Throughout the history of the Christian Church there has been controversy around the use of incense, with its regular use in some traditions and disapproval of it in others (Grisbrooke, 1986). Incense was first used in worship in the middle of the fourth century and has been a symbol of prayer in some Christian traditions ever since. In the Eucharist incense can be used to cense the altar, the Gospel book, the priest, and the people.

Fragrant oil was also part of sensing God. In Exodus, the Lord speaks to Moses:

> The Lord spoke to Moses: Take the finest spices: of liquid myrrh five hundred shekels, and of sweet-smelling cinnamon half as much, that is, two hundred and fifty, and two hundred and fifty of aromatic cane, and five hundred of cassia–measured by the sanctuary shekel–and a hin of olive oil. (Exodus 30.22–24)

The sense of smell was part of the ministry of Jesus. Mary, Lazarus' sister, honoured and worshipped Jesus in Bethany by offering a fragrant perfume to anoint him (John 12.3), an action that communicated extravagant devotion to Jesus.

Beth speaks to Paul and Maggie about the anointing of people at different stages of their Christian journey. She remembers in particular the anointing of her friends when they were ordained priest, and reflects on her experience of attending the Chrism Mass in her cathedral on Maundy Thursday, when the bishop blesses the oils for use in the churches. The word chrism comes from the Greek word meaning to anoint. People are anointed with oil mixed with balsam and other spices. The use of special oils for liturgical functions was evident in the Old Testament with the anointing of kings and priests. The first Christians in the Early Church took over this practice and anointed people at baptism, confirmation and ordination. Holy oil is also used for anointing the sick and the dying.

While the sense of smell within worship is not part of the ritual in every church, Ann Richards, working with the Mission Theological Advisory Group, claims that there is a distinctive smell associated with holiness and offering: 'When the people encounter the distinctive smell, they will know they are in a holy place and among holy things. They will be encouraged to think about God' (Richards, 2007, p. 49).

Tasting: the sense of taste

In the Bible the sense of taste was used to communicate to people. There is an encouragement to taste the sweetness of honey in Proverbs 23.13. In the Book of Revelation John writes of a similar experience of the taste of honey (Revelation 10.9).

The sense of taste is used in the Passover meal by the Jews as a remembrance of their time in slavery and the Passover of the Lord. Several foods are eaten to remind the people of God's deliverance: Matzos and bitter herbs symbolize the unleavened bread the

Israelites made and the bitterness of the slavery they endured.

The Eucharist or Mass was instituted on the night of the Passover and reminds people of the sacrifice of Jesus through the sharing of bread and wine.

> In the Eucharistic feeding, sharing and indwelling God's word, 'tasting' Jesus by means of the bread of life, all come together. The sharing of food relates not just to bodily need but to the memory of God's deeds and desire God's people to be saved and to be whole. Eating and drinking provokes prayer, praise and memory, so that human creatureliness is tied to God's intention. Moreover all the food and 'taste-experience' imagery of offering, sacrifice and bread of life, are gathered up in the Eucharist and focused on the gift of Christ's body and blood as our own particular feeding miracle expressed in fellowship and community. (Richards, 2007, p. 87)

As Paul, Beth and Maggie continue to reflect, Paul talks about his experience of the Seder meal on Maundy Thursday with the tasting of the bitter herbs and the flatbread. The service led in to the Lord's Supper and the sharing of bread, the body of Christ, and the wine, the blood of Christ. He thinks about the way food has been used to explain the act of remembrance and how taste can be used to express sweetness and joy as well as sadness and bitterness.

TO DO

Thinking of your own experience, how does smell and taste help you in worship and liturgy?

Can you think about a service you have attended that uses these senses to enhance your experience of God and your journey of faith?

Hearing: the sense of hearing

The sense of hearing has been the main sense used in worship particularly since the Reformation when services were to be conducted in the vernacular. Hearing the word of God, however understood, has been the focus in the Old and New Testaments. Hearing God's word was important to Moses, and to the psalmist. In the New Testament Jesus encourages his followers to hear his words. God's people hear God call and they respond (1 Samuel 3.10; Mark 1.16–20).

When most congregations were illiterate hearing the words was particularly important. As Christianity grew and the congregations and church buildings got bigger, intoning was introduced to enable more people to hear. When church services were carried out in a language that people could not understand it was important to know what was happening in the service by other means. In medieval times, when the Mass was recited in Latin, bells were rung at the important points in the service so that people were aware of what was going on. After the Reformation, with the doctrinal emphasis on the word, churches built large pulpits together with sounding boards so that the word of God could be heard.

Conclusion

This chapter has explored the senses in worship. It has looked at the development of liturgy and the role the senses have played. It has reflected on the Bible and the senses and the development of the sensory environment to enhance worship and liturgy.

Further reading

Bianchi, E., 2002, *Words of Spirituality*, London: SPCK.

Giles, R., 2004, *Creating Uncommon Worship*, Norwich: Canterbury Press

Gray-Reeves, M. and Perham, M., 2011, *The Hospitality of God: Emerging worship for a missional church*, London: SPCK

Hawes, Arthur (unpublished), *Sense and Non-sense in Worship*,www.spiritualjourneys.org.uk.

Perham, M., 1992, *Liturgy Pastoral and Parochial*, London: SPCK.

Poole, D. M., 2004, *Effectiveness of Multisensory Communication in Worship*, unpublished dissertation for the Degree Doctor of Ministry: Faculty of Asbury Theological Seminary.

Richards, A., 2007, *Sense Making Faith: Body, spirit, journey*, London: CTBI.

www.churchofengland.org/prayer-and-worship/
worship-texts-and-resources/common-worship/
churchs-year/times-and-seasons/lent#mmm133

References

Archbishops' Council, 2005, *Common Worship: Daily Prayer,* London: Church House Publishing.

Augustine, 1961, *Confessions* (translated by R. S. Pine-Coffin), London: Penguin.

Bianchi, E., 2002, *Words of Spirituality*, London: SPCK.

Billings, A., 2004, *Secular Lives, Sacred Hearts: The role of the church in a time of no religion*, London: SPCK.

Bradshaw, P., 1992, 'The Divine Office: first three centuries', in C. Jones, G. Wainwright, E. Yarnold and P. Bradshaw (eds.) in *The Study of Liturgy,* revised edition, pp. 399-403, London: SPCK.

Bradshaw, P., (ed), 2002, *Companion to Common Worship* Vol. 1, London: SPCK.

Bradshaw, P., (ed), 2006, *Companion to Common Worship* Vol. 2, London: SPCK.

Bradshaw, P., Giles, G. and Kershaw, S., 2002, 'Holy Communion', in P. Bradshaw, (ed.) *Companion to Common Worship,* Vol. 1, pp. 98–147, London: SPCK.

Buchanan, C., Lloyd, T. and Miller, H., 1980, *Anglican Worship Today*, London: Collins.

Burns, S., 2006, *Liturgy: SCM Studyguide*, London:

SCM Press.

Church of England, 1928, *The Book of Common Prayer: With the additions and deviations proposed in 1928*, Cambridge: Cambridge University Press.

Church of England, 1973, *An Order for Holy Communion: With music for the congregation*, London: SPCK.

Church of England, 1976, *Holy Communion, Series 1 & 2 (revised)*, London: SPCK.

Church of England, 1980, *The Alternative Service Book 1980*, London: Hodder and Stoughton.

Church of England, 1986, *Lent, Holy Week, Easter: Services and prayers*, London: SPCK.

Church of England, 1986, *The Promise of His Glory: For the season from All Saints to Candlemas*, London: SPCK.

Church of England, 1995, *On the Way: Towards an integrated approach to Christian Initiation* GS Misc 444. London, Church House Publishing.

Church of England, 2000, 2011 *Common Worship: Pastoral Services*, London: Church House Publishing.

Church of England, 2002, *New Patterns for Worship*, London: Church House Publishing.

Church of England, 2005, *Common Worship: Daily Prayer*, London: Church House Publishing.

Church of England, 2006, *Common Worship: Times and Seasons*, London, Church House Publishing.

Church of England Liturgical Commission, 2014,

Christian Initiation: Additional texts in Accessible Language GS1958, London, General Synod of the Church of England.

Church of the Province of New Zealand, 1989, *New Zealand Prayer Book,* Auckland: William Collins Publishers.

Crichton, J. D., 1991, 'Marriage', in J. G. Davies (ed), *A New Dictionary of Liturgy and Worship*, pp. 351–2, London: SCM Press.

Cuming, G. J., 1991, 'Marriage', in J. G. Davies (ed), *A New Dictionary of Liturgy and Worship*, pp. 352–3 London: SCM Press.

Cuming, G. J., 1992, 'The Office in the Anglican Communion', in C. Jones, G. Wainwright, E. Yarnold and P. Bradshaw (eds.), *The Study of Liturgy,* revised edition, pp. 441–6, London: SPCK.

Cummings, B., 2013, *The Book of Common Prayer: the texts of 1549, 1559, and 1662* (Oxford World's Classics), Oxford: Oxford University Press.

Dawtry, A., and Headley, C., 2001, 'A Service of the Word', P. Bradshaw (ed.), *Companion to Common Worship Vol 1,* pp. 52–84, London: SPCK.

Earey, M., Gay, P. and Horton, A., 2001, *Understanding Worship: A praxis study guide,* London: Mowbray.

Earey, M. and Myers, G., 2001, *Common Worship Today: an illustrated guide to common worship,* London: Harper Collins.

Everett, H., 2006, 'Marriage' in P. Bradshaw (ed.), *A Companion to Common Worship Volume 2*, pp. 180–193, London, SPCK.

Gelineau, J., 1992, 'Music and Singing in the Liturgy', in C. Jones, G. Wainwright, E. Yarnold, and P. Bradshaw (ed), *The Study of Liturgy, revised edition*, pp. 493–507, London: SPCK.

Giles, R., 1999, *Re-Pitching the Tent*, Norwich: Canterbury Press.

Giles, R., 2004, *Creating Uncommon Worship*, Norwich: Canterbury Press.

Giles, G., 2006, 'Funerals' in P. Bradshaw (ed.), *A Companion to Common Worship*, Vol. 2, pp. 194–218, London: SPCK.

Gordon-Taylor, B., 2002, 'The Calendar', in P. Bradshaw (ed), *Companion to Common Worship* Vol. 1, pp 38–46, London: SPCK.

Gray-Reeves, M. and Perham, M., 2011, *The Hospitality of God: Emerging worship for a missional church*, London: SPCK.

Grisbrooke, W. J., 1986, 'Incense', in J. G. Davies (ed), *A New Dictionary of Liturgy and Worship*, pp. 265-6, London: SCM Press.

Hawes, Arthur, unpublished, *Sense and Non-sense in worship*, www.spiritualjourneys.org.uk

Jasper, R. C. D. and Bradshaw, P. F., 1992, *A Companion to the Alternative Service Book*, London: SPCK.

Johnson, M. E. 2013, 'Initiation', in J. Day, and B. Gordon-Taylor (ed), *The Study of Liturgy and Worship*, pp. 125–134, London: SPCK.

Jones, S. and Tovey, P., 2002, 'Christian Initiation', in P. Bradshaw (ed.), *Companion to Common Worship*, pp. 148–78. London: SPCK.

Kelly, R. B., 1999, *Exploring the Sacraments*, Stowmarket: Kevin Mayhew.

Lloyd, T., 2013, 'Marriage' in, J. Day and B. Gordon-Taylor (eds), *The Study of Liturgy and Worship*, pp. 168–77, London, SPCK.

Maloney, R., 1995, *The Eucharist*, London: Geoffrey Chapman.

Methodist Church, 1999, *The Methodist Worship Book*, Peterborough: Methodist Publishing House.

Methodist Church (2003) *His Presence Makes the Feast: Holy Communion in the Methodist Church*, www.methodist.org.uk

Perham, M., 1992, *Liturgy, Pastoral and Parochial*, London: SPCK.

Perham, M., 2000, *New Handbook of Pastoral Liturgy*, London: SPCK.

Poole, D M., 2004, 'Effectiveness of Multisensory Communication in Worship', unpublished dissertation for the Doctor of Ministry Degree: Faculty of Asbury Theological Seminary.

Richards, A., 2007, *Sense Making Faith: Body, spirit, journey*, London: CTBI

Richardson, A., 1993, 'Worship' in A. Richardson and J. Bowden (eds.), *A New Dictionary of Christian Theology*, pp. 605-6, London: SCM Press.

Sinclair, J., 2002, 'The Psalter' in P. Bradshaw (ed.), *Companion to Common Worship*, pp. 236-8, London: SPCK.

Society of St Francis, 1992, *Celebrating Common Prayer*, London: Mowbray.

Tripp, D. H.,1992, 'The Office in the Lutheran, Reformed and Free Churches' in C. Jones, G. Wainwright, E. Yarnold and P. Bradshaw (eds), *The Study of Liturgy*, revised edition, pp. 447-54, London: SPCK.

Wesley, J., 1784, *The Sunday Service*, London: Kershaw.

Wesley J., 1788, *The Sunday Services of the Methodists with other occasional services*. London: Kershaw.

Wesley J., 1889, *Collection of Hymns for the use of the people called Methodists,* London: Wesleyan-Methodist book-room.

Wesley J., and Wesley, C., 1825, *Hymns of the Lord's Supper*, London: Kershaw

White, J. F., 2000, *Introducing Christian Worship*, Nashville TN: Abingdon Press.

White, S. J., 1997, *Groundwork of Christian Worship*, Peterborough: Epworth Press.